GARDNER

A DREAM COME TRUE

A BIOGRAPHY BY NICK HARTGERINK

HUTCHINSON AUSTRALIA

Century Hutchinson Australia Pty Ltd
20 Alfred Street, Milsons Point, New South Wales 2061

Sydney Melbourne London
Auckland Johannesburg
and agencies throughout the world

First published 1989
Reprinted November 1989

Copyright © Newland Ltd, 1989

National Library of Australia
Cataloguing-in-Publication Data

Hartgerink, Nick.
  Gardner, a dream come true.

  ISBN 0 09 169580 5.

  1. Gardner, Wayne, 1959-   . 2. Motorcyclists
  - Australia - Biography. I. Title.

796.7'5'0924

Designed and typeset by Midland Typesetters, Maryborough
Printed by Globe Press, Melbourne
Production by Vantage Graphics, Sydney

Contents

Author's Acknowledgement

Many people have contributed to these pages by willingly giving me their time and their memories during my research. They are too numerous to name, but will themselves know how much they have enhanced the book. I am grateful to them all. Thanks are also due to the many photographers whose pictures we have used.

A few people deserve special mention: Wayne's mother Shirley, father Norm and sister Vicki, for filling in the gaps from Wayne's early years and giving me full access to all the family albums and scrapbooks; Donna Forbes for her encouragement and honesty; Harris Barnett for his considerable and much-appreciated support; and my wife Jayne, who provided valued appraisal of each chapter and carried more than her share of family responsibilities while I worked on the book.

However, the person who deserves the highest praise is Wayne Gardner himself. He gave generously of his precious time throughout my research, and insisted that we tell his story 'warts and all'—which is as it should be. But more than that, watching him achieve what he has over the past thirteen years has been an inspiration to me. He is a true champion, and it is a great honour for me to tell his life story.

Nick Hartgerink

Wayne Gardner's Acknowledgement

So many people have helped me throughout my career that I should start at the beginning. My parents got me started in racing and, along with my sister Vicki, have always given me the best possible family support. Donna, too, has always been there to help me enjoy the good times and get me through the hard times, while I simply don't know what I would have done without my manager, Harris Barnett. Many people have helped my racing over the years. Kevin Cass was my first sponsor, followed by Karl and Willi Praml and Kevin Fraser. Then came Billy Hill, his partner Phil Kostic, and Peter Molloy. Mamoru Moriwaki took me overseas and has been available for guidance ever since, while Roger Marshall has been a special friend. My team managers with Honda—Barry Symmonds, Jerry Burgess and Stuart Shenton—have all played a major role in any success I've had, while Wilf Needham has been much more than my mechanic over the past nine years. Others to whom I owe a special debt are Dr Claudio Costa, for getting me back on the track despite injuries that should have kept me out much longer; Phil Fearon; and the author of this book, Nick Hartgerink, who has followed and supported my career from the beginning. I thank them all. I couldn't have achieved anything without their help, support and friendship.

Wayne Gardner

Introduction

'I can't begin to express how I felt when I came around the back of the circuit and thousands of people had spilled out across the track to cheer me. I was crying inside my helmet, and I guess my tears said it all. I had won my country's first Grand Prix, and I couldn't quite believe it. It was a dream come true. When I was a kid I dreamed of becoming world motorcycle champion and that came true in 1987. When I heard Australia was getting a Grand Prix I started dreaming of winning that too. To actually do it is almost too good to be true.'

Wayne Gardner, after winning the inaugural
Australian 500-cc Grand Prix, Phillip Island,
9 April 1989

The doctor had just left Wayne Gardner in his hotel room at the Suzuka Circuit, Japan. The diagnosis was a relief; he wouldn't need to have his left testicle removed. But the pain was intense—an excruciating reminder of his mistake in the Japanese Grand Prix the previous day. He had run off the circuit and been flung into the air, crashing down on his motorcycle's tank with sickening impact. Somehow he had regained control before the machine slammed into a wall, and had rejoined the race to finish a courageous fourth in the opening race of the 1989 500-cc world championship.

Gardner pondered the cause and effect of a riding performance which he considered his worst for years. Twice he had come through the field, only to run off the circuit each time and throw away a certain rostrum finish. He was disgusted, and had a very bruised and swollen reminder of how poorly he'd ridden. But more than that, he knew he had to do something drastic to lift himself for the race he wanted to win more than any other before it—Australia's first 500-cc world championship Grand Prix two weeks later. That the race was being staged at all was a tribute to Gardner's phenomenal international success. When he left Australia in 1981 to chase a racing career overseas, Gardner and motorcycle racing had meant nothing to Australians. Now he was returning as a hero in a sport he had switched a whole country on to. He desperately wanted to win to bring the story full circle.

Gardner was under intense pressure—some self-inflicted by nerves from his burning ambition to win his country's first Grand Prix, and the rest heaped on him by Honda's decision secretly to sign his arch rival, American Eddie Lawson, and pit the world's two best riders against each other on the same bikes. Gardner knew that was why he had ridden so badly in Japan, and he was determined it wasn't going to happen in Australia.

Sitting in his hotel room that morning, Gardner came up with a solution. He decided to go back to his roots. He wanted to shrug off the entourage that always seems to surround top sportsmen. His team personnel seemed to grow every year, and he was embarrassed by its burgeoning number. In Japan, even for breakfast in the hotel dining room, at least ten people tagged along. He felt like a pampered poodle, and didn't enjoy it one bit. He wanted to go back to being what he had started out as all those years before—just a guy who jumps on his bike and wrings its neck as hard as he can. If he was going home to show his country why he had won a world championship, he wanted to go back to being a racer—nothing more, nothing less. The solution was simple: his sports psychologist would be sent home to England; his physiotherapist would be told to come only when called for and stop fussing over him every minute of the day; his friends and even family would be warned that he had a job to do and he'd see them when it was done.

Gardner had to win the Australian Grand Prix, it was as simple as that. When he did, no-one should have been surprised. All his life Wayne Gardner has been setting himself goals and achieving them.

CHAPTER I

Just a Larrikin Kid

Every neighbourhood has one—a kid who is a little braver, or crazier, than the others, a kid who is prepared to take risks. One who doesn't mind getting hurt, or ripping his clothes, as long as he is having fun. A kid who drags the others along with him in increasingly daring escapades. One who is a hero to other children but not necessarily to parents, who fear that the next adventure may end in disaster. A cheeky kid who doesn't have a great respect for rules—or the law.

Back around 1970 Balgownie had such a kid. Balgownie was a suburb that had grown from a coalmining village into a residential area for the miners and steelworkers of the industrial heartland of Wollongong on the New South Wales south coast, just eighty kilometres from Sydney. Its people were solidly working class—steelworkers, coalminers, truck drivers and labourers. Balgownie had a mixture of modest, well-kept homes with a sprinkling of light industry on the fringes. Balgownie was the sort of suburb and community you'd find near major industrial centres just about anywhere in the world, although few industrial towns enjoy such a marvellous position, flanked as it is by a magnificent bush-clad escarpment to the west and the blue Pacific Ocean just two kilometres to the east.

While there was nothing special about Balgownie, it did have Wayne Gardner, a fact it is immensely proud of now. And yet it is doubtful whether anyone outside the Gardner family thought he'd amount to much back in the 1970s. You see, Wayne Gardner was one of *those* kids. There is a marvellous word to describe kids like him: he was a larrikin—a likeable rogue who didn't go looking for trouble but often managed to find it anyway.

Young Wayne was born on 11 October 1959. From an early age he showed a remarkable desire, a craving, for speed. It was all he lived for. He had to go faster and faster, even on his dinky tricycle. Not much else mattered. And in many ways, not much else matters today. One thing that did matter, though, was a challenge. If anybody told him something couldn't or shouldn't be done, he would set about proving them wrong. That has been a driving force behind his whole career. For one so successful, he has always been plagued by an inordinate number of doubters, and he has delighted in proving them wrong.

Alan Bond's 1987 Swan Premium Lager television commercial featuring Gardner, which started off: 'They said you'd never make it, you were just a larrikin kid', was much more than a smart advertising jingle. It summed up Gardner's entire career, from the Auto Cycle Union officials who wanted to take away his racing licence when he was a rookie, to the Australian motorcycle press and then the British who thought he had no future, on to ex-champions such as Barry Sheene who stated publicly that Gardner didn't have what it took to be a world champion. Their barbs hurt Gardner, because he is much more sensitive than you would imagine a fearless 300-kilometre-per-hour motorcycle racer to be. But they also spurred him on. Anyone who said Wayne Gardner wouldn't make it had to be proved wrong.

But back in 1970 the only ones who had to be proved wrong were the neighbourhood children who said no-one could ride the 300 metres of Breda Street, Balgownie, on the back wheel of their bicycle. Gardner thought he could, and practised for weeks until he did it.

'I guess I was a bit of a daredevil. I'd try anything, especially if anybody said it couldn't be done. That was like a red rag to a bull,' Gardner remembers. 'A new housing estate was being developed behind our home, and there was a huge hill with a road down it. The road wasn't finished and had rocks all over it, and nobody dared ride their bikes down it. I had a go—no hands! Of course I crashed and landed on my face. I was always doing that. I always had

4

skin off some part of my face. Mum was always having to patch me up.'

Gardner's mother Shirley still wonders how she survived those years. 'Wayne really was a little wretch. He'd always be doing things he wasn't supposed to,' she says. 'His father Norm had a truck in those days, and Wayne liked to help him work on it on the weekends. Norm would have the tipper up and be working underneath, and Wayne would climb into the cabin and play with the controls. Next thing you'd know, he'd be lowering the tipper down on his father's head. Another time I found him dazed and semiconscious under his bed. He'd stuck a screwdriver in the electric power point to see what would happen. I felt sick for days thinking how close he'd come to electrocuting himself.'

Gardner's younger sister Vicki remembers similar incidents. 'Once he called me over to the barbecue. I looked in to see a plastic container of petrol that Wayne had put in amongst the flames. The plastic was starting to melt and we ran for it. The barbecue blew up in a ball of flame which destroyed Mum's banana trees. Another time Wayne had a plan to take Dad's ute out for a drive, because he'd been learning to drive it at the quarry where Dad worked and wanted to see if he could drive it on the road. I said he didn't even have a key, but Wayne said he knew how to get it going without a key. He would only have been about fourteen then.'

Gardner was fascinated with anything mechanical, from an early age destroying his toys as he dismantled them to see how they worked. Most times they wouldn't go back together again. For his tenth birthday, his parents gave him his first watch. Within a day it was in pieces on the kitchen table, never to work again.

'We bought a new lawn-mower,' Shirley Gardner remembers. 'We hadn't even used it before I found Wayne in the garage with the mower in a hundred pieces around him. I knew his father would be furious, but Wayne said he'd get it back together again. When he had finished there were five bolts left over, but it started up anyway, so we hid the bolts and Norm was never any the wiser.'

Inevitably, Gardner's dual passion for speed and things mechanical led him to engines that would propel him faster than a pushbike. A friend, Phillip Birch, had a go-kart, so Gardner pestered his father until he got one too. He was thirteen at the time, and Norm Gardner built the go-kart from scrap steel and a Victa 125-cc lawn-mower engine.

'My friend and I used to drive everyone crazy, driving around and around in a cul-de-sac in an industrial area near our home. Sometimes we used to take them on the streets, and the police used to chase us. They never caught me, but they knew where I was coming from, so once or twice they visited my parents,' he says, with a hint of a smile. 'Once I'd learned how to drive it, I was always looking for new and interesting things to do on it. We'd go down to the local school [Fairy Meadow Public School] on Saturday mornings and drive around all the paths. If they'd mown the grass we'd pile it up and drive through it like stuntmen, or empty the rotten fruit out of the rubbish bins and use it to skid on. That was always fun.

'One Saturday morning the headmaster came down in his car and chased us all over the school, which was pretty funny at the time. Another Saturday morning the police came and chased me up the street. I ducked into the entrance to the drive-in theatre and hid under the trees for half an hour until they had stopped looking for me. I was always in that go-kart, and Mum wouldn't give me enough money for petrol for all the driving I wanted to do. So my friends and I used to go down to the industrial area, climb the fences, and pinch the copper and brass fittings from the cranes and other machines that were parked there. We'd take them to the scrap metal merchant and cash them in. I did that for years, to buy petrol for the go-kart and later the motorcycles. I guess I'm not too proud of that now, but at the time it was a bit of a laugh. We looked on it as a bit if a necessity—it was the only way we could figure to raise the petrol money.'

It was on one of these scouting expeditions through

the local industrial areas that Gardner came across a find that was to change his life—and ultimately lead him to fame, fortune and a world championship. Gardner and a friend, Barry Sisson, spotted an old wreck of a motorcycle in a junk heap at the back of a factory. After plucking up the courage, they approached the factory manager and asked if they could buy it.

'It was a rusted heap of junk,' Gardner says. 'It was half buried, the engine was seized and rusted up and it had no back wheel. It was a Yamaha 80 agricultural bike, and must have been sitting there for donkey's years. But we reckoned we could fix it up so we eventually got up the nerve to ask the factory manager if we could buy it. He only wanted beer money and said we could have it for five dollars, so off we went home to our moneyboxes to get two-fifty each. I told my Mum what I was doing and she said I was a nut case. Then I asked her if she could go and get it in the car, which was the next piece of bad news. She must have been really embarrassed going to pick it up, and we travelled home with me sitting in the boot holding on to the bike.'

CHAPTER 2

Leader of the Pack

It didn't take long to get the bike into running order. Barry Sisson's father was an engineer and took the rusted engine away to be machined and cleaned up. Norm Gardner advertised in the local paper for a back wheel and picked one up for ten dollars. Never mind that it was off a Honda 250. It fitted, after a few modifications. The bike wasn't the prettiest, but looks didn't worry Gardner. At age thirteen, he had a motorcycle!

There were a few other neighbourhood boys with motorcycles, and soon Gardner had joined the pack, spending every afternoon riding the creekbeds behind his house or venturing along the fire trails up into the bushland of the escarpment behind Balgownie. Sharing the bike with his friend was difficult—both boys wanted to ride it at once—so Barry's father bought him a red 70-cc Honda for his birthday. Gardner bought out his friend's share of the hybrid Yamaha. 'It wasn't very flash, but I didn't care,' he remembers. 'The other boys' bikes were generally newer and smarter than mine but I just thought I was king of the block with my own motorcycle. I was on it every afternoon, and I made sure that anything they could do on their newer bikes, I could do better on mine.' The now-famous Gardner competitive spirit had manifested itself at an early age. 'When we first started riding in the creekbed, the big challenge was to ride down one side, through the water and up the other side. I landed in the water plenty of times, but I mastered it.'

Perhaps surprisingly, Gardner still talks with pride of small achievements such as riding through creekbeds, or wheelstanding his bicycle down Breda Street. It is obvious that nothing is taken lightly, that no milestone is forgotten. Everything is stored away, to be drawn on when the need arises. All things are relative of course, and perhaps at thirteen Gardner had to draw on the same reserves of courage and determination to master the creekbed crossing as he needs today to beat Eddie Lawson and company in a Grand Prix. He's the same with people. A warm, caring and surprisingly soft person to those he cares about, he can be uncompromisingly hard about people he dislikes, or who he considers have 'dudded' him. And he never forgets.

It soon became obvious to Norm and Shirl Gardner that their son was becoming obsessed with his motorcycle. The machine spent every night in Wayne's bedroom—after sister Vicki had been press-ganged into helping push it up the back steps and down the hallway, with the handlebars generally scraping off the wallpaper on the way. Inevitably, school homework was being ignored as Wayne and his friends rode their bikes until nightfall, then collapsed exhausted into bed. Finally, Norm Gardner put his foot down.

'Norm decided the only way to stop Wayne riding the bike was to chain it up in the garage on certain days, and he would have to do his homework instead of going out on it,' Shirley Gardner recalls. 'We thought this was working, until one afternoon when I came home and smelt petrol in the garage. I felt the bike's engine and it was hot, so I knew Wayne had somehow got the bike out despite the chain and padlock. Wayne claimed he had just been revving the engine in the garage, but I felt the tyres and they were warm, so he had obviously been out on it. To this day Wayne has refused to tell me how he did it, but he did. That was the trouble with him as a kid—say something couldn't be done, and he'd find a way. It nearly drove me mad then, but it is clear to me now that is why he has been so successful in racing. He just doesn't know when he is beaten.'

Still, he was beaten that day. When Norm Gardner got home and heard that Wayne had managed to unchain the bike, he grounded his son for a week. To make sure the punishment stuck, Norm removed the bike's back wheel and took it with him to work each day. Norm Gardner, however, could see a certain inevitability in the situation, and for Christmas he bought his son a new bike—a Yamaha GTMX80.

'It cost $299, which was a lot of money in those days, and I loved it,' Gardner recalls. 'I thought it was pretty racy,

9

so of course I had to get a loud exhaust, and I even put castor oil in the petrol to make it smell like racing fuel. I always had the engine apart, seeing how the whole thing worked. Mind you, I was a bit more careful by this stage because when I had the agricultural bike, I had taken the gearbox apart and couldn't put it together again. It took us weeks to track down a manual with some drawings in to show us what to do. But by this stage my friends had graduated to XR75s—which were the business in those days—and I was always working on my GTMX80 to make it go as fast as the XR75s.'

Young Wayne seemed to have racing in his blood, and at the end of 1973 he persuaded his father to allow him to join Wollongong and Districts Motorcycle Training Club. At the time, children under the age of sixteen were not allowed to race in New South Wales, but the club got around that without any problems. Led by Dave Horton, a large, effusive man described by Gardner as 'a bigger kid than all the kids he was looking after', the club organised regular family days at an old dirt airstrip near Wilton, about thirty kilometres west of Wollongong. There were no 'races'. It just so happened that groups of boys on mini-bikes rode as fast as they could against each other around a designated circuit.

Gardner's first memory of racing at Wilton was a father-and-son race. 'The kids had to do three laps, then hand over to their fathers who did three laps, then we'd take over again, and so on,' says Gardner. 'Dad had never been on a bike before so I told him just to jump on and hold the throttle wide open. I was coming about third or fourth when I handed it over to Dad, and he jumped on and grabbed the throttle. The bike took off with a big wheelie, throwing him off the back. But he kept hold of the throttle as the bike dragged him all over the place, even knocking down two mothers who were watching the race.' It must have looked hilarious, but even now in retelling it Gardner fails to see much humour in the incident. He was much more concerned that his father had cost them vital placings in the race, and worse, damaged the bike. Norm Gardner says he was surprised at his son's reaction. 'I gashed my elbow quite badly but Wayne didn't even notice; he was too concerned about his bike and went running after it to check whether it could still be ridden in the race. I knew then that we had a son with a competitive spirit a bit more developed than most,' Norm says.

From the informal competition at Wilton, Gardner moved on to observed trials at Menai on Sydney's southern outskirts. He had also graduated to a Yamaha TY80. Observed trials are individual tests of control of a motorcycle, where riders must pass through sections of obstacle courses. Speed is incidental. Rather, points are deducted if the riders put their feet on the ground or a wheel outside the designated course. It is excellent training for learning to control a motorcycle, but somewhat boring if you happen to be born with speed in your veins.

'It used to wind me up, going so slow,' Gardner recalls. 'I would complete each section, then absolutely fang the bike to the next section—dirt-tracking, sliding, and arriving at the next checkpoint in a cloud of dust. The TY80 was geared down so it could climb over the obstacles, and it would only do about thirty miles [fifty kilometres] an hour flat-out. But I used to make sure it was doing that between every section. I couldn't handle going so slow in those tiny sections. It was so frustrating, and the emotion used to build up in me so that I'd just go for it between each one.' Even now, all these years later as he retells the story, Gardner still displays all the pent-up aggression he must have felt at the time—a kid who knew only one speed: flat-out.

Gardner met his first world motorcycle champion at Menai, when he attended a training school conducted by the then world trials champion, Englishman Mick Andrews.

'Mick was really nice to me, but I don't think he thought I had much of a future in trials competition. He probably just thought I was a cheeky kid who liked to fang bikes. I suppose he heard the news when I won the world championship in 1987, but I wonder if he ever realised it was the same kid who attended his training school.'

The flirtation with trials didn't last long. Gardner wanted to go racing. Dave Horton suggested they start travelling to Canberra, where regulations allowed fifteen year olds to compete in organised racing. Norm Gardner bought Wayne a YZ80 Yamaha, and a racing career was born.

Wayne headed for Canberra every weekend he could.

Sometimes Norm would pack the YZ80 into the back of his utility truck for the three-hour drive, while other times Wayne would squeeze into Dave Horton's battered old Chrysler station wagon, loaded down with mini-bikes on the roof-rack and in a trailer and five or six teenage boys.

'I'll never forget those trips with Dave. The car was always piled high with bikes and kids, and there were spark plugs and chain links and other bits and pieces all over the place—a real junk shop. And Dave used to drive like a frigging lunatic, frightening us half to death. But it was a heap of fun,' Gardner says.

In Canberra Wayne revelled in the racing, particularly the short-circuit competition on a circular, flat track of hard-packed dirt—similar to flat-track racing in the United States. He also tried his hand at motocross, but found that almost as frustrating as observed trials. 'Motocross didn't suit me; there was too much jumping and stopping and starting. All I wanted to do was go flat-out.'

On free weekends, Wayne would strap a spare petrol can onto his bike and head up along the fire trails in the bush west of Wollongong. 'There was always a heap of us, and we'd spend the day out in the bush. Some of the guys were more interested in sitting around smoking pot, but all I wanted to do was ride. I was always pushing myself, trying new things. I never wanted to go home, and I'd stay out until it got dark.' Indeed, Wayne's obsession with riding knew no barriers, including pain barriers. 'I broke my leg once, when I was about fifteen, but didn't even stop then. I had been riding down a hill when one of my friends stopped at the bottom. I couldn't stop in time and slid into him, squashing my leg between the two bikes. My leg really hurt but I didn't want to go home, so I kept riding bikes all day. When I got home my leg was about this big [showing a lump the size of a tennis ball below his knee] and Mum rushed me off to hospital in a panic. It turned out I had a fracture—not a bad one, but a fracture all the same—and I'd ridden all day on it.'

Gardner says he was simply gamer than the other kids then, and perhaps he still is gamer than his rivals. In 1988 he raced in the Italian Grand Prix at Imola with six broken bones in his left foot after he crashed while testing in Yugoslavia the previous week. He kept the injury secret before the race to make sure he wasn't ruled medically unfit, and still rode superbly for second place despite intense pain. Later in the same season he raced in Sweden with displaced vertebrae after injuring his back in a heavy fall while qualifying. Once again, despite the pain, he finished a fighting second.

By 1974, after a year of riding, Wayne finished second in the Australian mini-bike titles and went looking for other challenges—ones that offered more speed. Wollongong Honda dealer Kevin Fraser offered him the use of a 125-cc machine for a dirt-track meeting at Lithgow, two and a half hours' drive west of Wollongong. 'It was a CR125 Honda—a big silver thing—and I remember when I brought it home my Mum said "no way", I couldn't ride it, because it was too big and too powerful,' Gardner recalls.

His mother Shirley says, 'I was dead against it. Wayne couldn't even touch the ground with his feet when he was sitting on it. I thought he was much too young to ride a bike that size but he wouldn't take "no" for an answer, so off he went to Lithgow. He had six races on the bike that day, and won all six, so there wasn't much I could say after that.' Gardner was hooked, and, soon afterwards, bought himself a Yamaha YZ125.

For the next two years, Gardner won just about everything there was to enter; but, more importantly, dirt-track racing saw him develop a technique that was to propel him to the forefront of world championship road racing more than a decade later. He was learning the art of rear-wheel steering. The technique involves sensitive throttle control to feed power to a sliding rear wheel which *pushes* the bike through and out of a corner, rather than the so-called 'classic' line where a rider *glides* through a corner. Such a technique is second nature to dirt racers, but Gardner was later to adapt it to tar, where the advantages are considerable because a rider can start feeding the horsepower to the rear wheel much earlier in the exit from the corner than his rival taking the classic, sweeping arc through the curve. A rider can dive deep into a corner, leaving his braking until the last possible moment, then with one savage motion can throw his bike sideways and power out of the corner using throttle control to his still-sliding rear tyre to propel him in the desired direction. It isn't as pretty to watch as a classic line through a corner, but it is much more effective. As any Grand Prix racer will tell, exit speed from a corner is critical in attaining maximum speed as quickly as possible down the straight, and the rear-wheel steerers can get power to the ground faster than anybody else.

Three-times world champion Californian Kenny Roberts brought the technique to world championship road racing in 1978 when he came to Europe to begin his three-year reign at the top. He had developed it from flat-track racing back home, and it took the European riders completely by surprise. Even now, only a handful of riders, including Gardner and the top Americans such as Eddie Lawson, Randy Mamola and Freddie Spencer, have mastered it completely. It is no coincidence that they have dominated the sport in the last decade. Nevertheless, Gardner could hardly have anticipated that what he learned on dirt in Lithgow or Queanbeyan in front of 100 mums and dads could possibly have given him the winning edge in front of 100,000 fans at Grand Prix tracks all over the world.

At the end of 1976 a Wollongong Motorcycle Club member, John Zammit, persuaded Gardner to try his hand at road racing. Wayne put road tyres on his 125-cc Yamaha dirt bike, changed the gearing and headed to Oran Park Raceway on Sydney's south-western outskirts to try his hand at a new challenge. He came second in his first race, for 125-cc machines, so entered a 250-cc event. 'I knew I needed more power. I noticed everyone had their air filters off to help them go faster, so I took mine off my bike. I didn't know anything about enriching the [oil/petrol] mixture to take into account the extra air getting in, and after a couple of laps the engine seized while I was going down the main straight. I didn't know anything about seizures, and how I should have pulled in the clutch, so I just came to a grinding halt leaving a skid mark four miles long. I ended up right in front of the control tower and pit lane—very embarrassing!'

After the races had finished Zammit allowed Gardner to take his TZ250 Yamaha Grand Prix racer out onto the track for a few laps. 'I remember coming round onto the main straight for the first time and winding it up. I was like a missile—like an FA18 jet. I couldn't get over it. I'd never felt anything like it, an unbelievable sensation, as though my arms were going to be pulled out of my shoulders. The more I felt it the more I wanted it, and I started to go faster and faster. John was getting a bit nervous about me crashing, and pulled me in. He told me I'd been just a second or two off the C grade lap record, and that pumped me up even more. I was convinced this was what I wanted. Something inside me told me, "This is it, this is the way to go." '

Gardner went home, 'threw the 125 in the corner' and told his father he had to go road racing. 'I wanted to make a profession out of it. I had been studying the motorcycle magazines and I could see road racing got a lot more publicity than any other branch of the sport. More publicity means more money and better sponsorships. Even at 17 I was looking at it like a business. I didn't know anything about road racing but I was convinced it was the way to go, so I started looking around for a second-hand TZ.'

CHAPTER 3

Working-class Man

I n 'Steeltown', Australia, in the mid-seventies, teenagers could only *dream* of careers as sporting heroes. Wollongong kids mostly left school as soon as they could and applied for a job in the steelworks or the coalmines. Wayne Gardner was no different. His father wanted him to have a trade, so he left Keira Boys' High School at sixteen and applied to join the steelworks. He was happy to leave school, feeling that it generally served no useful purpose. He disliked academic subjects, and remembers being involved in 'heaps of fights'.

'I was always coming home with blood on my clothes from a fight. I don't know why—I guess I was cheeky, and would stand up to the bigger kids. They used to call me "The Fly". I got the cane a lot from the teachers too. I got picked on by the other kids and the teachers—I guess because I was a little smart-arse.' Gardner remembers a running battle with his art teacher with particular relish. 'He always wanted us to draw mountains and people and that sort of thing. I hated that, and I'd always be drawing motorcycles. He'd lecture me on how foolish I was, saying there was no future in motorcycles, that I'd never amount to anything if I was only interested in motorcycles.'

Gardner sat for the steelworks entrance exam but missed out. 'I don't know, I guess I was too dumb,' he laughs. 'But the worst thing was I had to go back to school at the beginning of the next year.' He lasted another five weeks before applying for an apprenticeship in fitting, turning and boilermaking at Tubemakers, manufacturers of welded steel pipes with a big plant at Kembla Grange, near Wollongong. This time he was lucky, and landed the job.

Gardner was earning the princely sum of $48 per week, with $25 of that going towards paying off a loan to his father for a TZ250 racer he bought early in 1977. That didn't leave much to live on, and Gardner made things worse by toting up regular speeding fines in his Holden utility. Shirley Gardner remembers with dread her son's early days as a driver: 'Wayne was always getting booked for speeding, and pretty soon the police started to look out for him. The ute started out blue, and at one stage Wayne painted it chocolate brown so the police wouldn't recognise him.' The Wollongong highway patrol wised up pretty soon, and Wayne had his licence cancelled so many times that it took him four years to advance beyond the probationary stage.

In those days Wollongong had its own 'hot-rod strip' at South Beach, where likely lads in their hotted-up cars would gather on Friday and Saturday nights to burn out their tyres and try to outdo each other with acts of motorised bravado. A favourite pastime was to spread oil on the roadway and skid or spin on it. Wayne was drawn to the action like a moth to flame. 'I was a lunatic in the car. I always had to be going sideways in it, and I loved going down to South Beach and doing doughnuts [spins]. Or we'd drive onto playing fields at night and slide and spin and do all sorts of things on the wet grass. I was possessed with needing to go sideways—it was quite ridiculous. I don't know how I wasn't killed but maybe it was a natural ability to control it that got me through.' More often than not Wayne would have a girl in the front seat of the ute, and be trying desperately to impress her with increasingly daring manoeuvres. No, the teenage Wayne Gardner was not a model citizen. A likeable one, maybe, but not a model one. His mother says: 'I suppose you'd have to say he was a bit of a bugger of a kid in some ways, but he was a great kid too. He'd do anything for you. You could never stay cross with him for long.'

Gardner had started to get serious about his racing. Like everything, he pitched straight into the deep end, choosing Amaroo Park in Sydney for his debut. It's a short, tight track circled by rock walls. Wollongong Yamaha dealer and Gardner's first sponsor, Kevin Cass, warned him not to race there until he had more experience because it was too dangerous, but Gardner ignored him. 'I went straight into a C-grade race and came second, so I came home thinking I was pretty good. I went into Cass's shop and said "I did it, I did it, I told you so." '

His next race meeting was at Oran Park. After winning the 250-cc C-grade race, Gardner decided he could tackle the 350-cc riders. It ended in disaster. 'I was running second and chasing the leader, and I was getting a little bit too cocky for myself. I was chasing pretty hard and looking good to win it, but of course I didn't know anything about bikes sliding or pitching you off. Sure enough, it pitched me off at Sutton's Corner, high-siding me real good. I landed heavily on my head and shoulder, and thought "Shit, what happened to me? Did you get the number of that truck that hit me?". It really did frighten me and hurt me, and I remember walking over to the wall to get out of the way of the other bikes. When I put my hands on the wall to jump over it I collapsed in pain. A guy came over and asked me what was wrong, and I said my shoulder was sore. He zipped off my leathers and there was a big lump on my shoulder. He said I must have broken my collarbone, and I said, "What the hell's a collarbone?".'

Perhaps it was a blessing that the seventeen year old didn't know much about anatomy, because the injury certainly didn't deter him. Within five weeks Gardner was back racing, and he quickly progressed to provisional B grade during the 1977 season. He was spending all his money on racing—paying his father back for the bike, buying tyres and parts, and travelling to race meetings. So his first prize money, insignificant by today's standards, was more than welcome. In May 1977 he won $25 for winning a race at Lakeside in Brisbane, and Shirley Gardner remembers that her son was so delighted that he didn't cash the cheque for weeks. 'He was so thrilled he didn't want to part with it. Eventually we compromised by taking a photocopy of it. Wayne just couldn't believe that he'd actually won some money from racing.' The photocopy still holds pride of place amongst the photos and press clippings in Shirley Gardner's extensive record of her son's career.

Back in his junior dirt-racing days Wayne had been tagged the Wollongong Wild One, and he was certainly living up to his nickname in road racing. He was either winning or crashing, and the sport's administrators were starting to get concerned. At the beginning of the 1978 season the New South Wales Auto Cycle Union road racing sub-committee was so concerned by his devil-may-care approach to racing that they were considering suspending him. Gardner's new sponsor, Wollongong motorcycle dealer Karl Praml, was a member of that sub-committee and remembers going to a meeting to apply for his rider to be promoted to full B grade status. Instead of approval, Praml was shocked to discover the rest of the sub-committee wanting Gardner banned for dangerous riding. 'They thought he was a danger to himself and everyone else on the track, and they wanted to put him out for six months,' Praml recalls. 'I begged for them to give Wayne another chance, which they finally agreed to, as long as I took him under control.'

Praml laid down the law to his spirited young charge, and instructed him not to win a race for six months. 'Wayne's problem was that he couldn't stand anyone being in front of him. If he wasn't winning he'd do everything in his power to get in front. He couldn't handle being second; he had to be in front. He'd either win the race or crash in the trying. I told him he'd have to learn to race properly, which meant finishing each time, and said if he won a race in the next six months I'd end the sponsorship. Wayne got super-snarly about it, but I eventually convinced him I wasn't joking and he settled down and started riding sensibly.'

Gardner remembers the time well. 'I was shocked when Karl told me the ACU was going to stop me racing,' he says. 'I just had no respect for the safety aspect of it. All I was interested in was winning. I thought that was all there was to racing—you went as hard as you could because first was the only place to finish. I must admit it set me back on my heels a bit to realise I was considered a danger. I was angry at first, but once I started riding a bit more slowly and making sure I finished, I began to learn a lot more about what the bike was doing and what I could do on it. It was my first real lesson in racing, and it was an important one. I still live by that motto now. It is better to finish second than to be sitting at the side of the track after a crash, watching everyone else go round.'

The new-look Gardner was quickly promoted to full B grade, and Praml decided to loosen the shackles. 'We were racing at Amaroo Park and Wayne was entered in an A-grade and a B-grade race with all the stars of the day—Warren Willing, Gary

Coleman, Vaughn Coburn and some other pretty hot riders,' Praml
recalls. 'We told Wayne he could go for it. I remember saying:
"You reckon you're good, then go ahead and prove it", but he
was nervous as a kitten. He got off the grid about tenth, but
put his head down and rode beautifully. Coleman was leading
from Willing, and Wayne came up behind him but was too scared
to overtake. Willing was the biggest name in Australia at that
stage and Wayne couldn't bring himself to go past him. He
eventually did though, and finished second to Coleman. When
he came in he was crying, he was so happy.'

The tears have continued to flow throughout Gardner's
career. He endeared himself to millions of Australians when
television beamed images of him standing in tears on the rostrum
at Goiania, Brazil, after clinching his first world championship
in September 1987. It showed just how much that title meant
to him. He cried when he won his first world championship Grand
Prix in Spain in April 1986, and when he arrived home to a hero's
welcome from 10,000 Wollongong people as the newly crowned
world champion in 1987. By then it was considered a genuine
and commendable emotion for a sportsman who had put in ten
hard years to reach the top and had achieved his dream. But
back in 1978, it hadn't been quite so acceptable. Bursting into
tears at the drop of a hat didn't fit the image of motorcycle racers
who risked their necks at high speeds.

'Wayne had a bit of a reputation as a wimp,' Karl Praml's
wife and team manager Willi says. 'That wasn't quite fair, because
he was a bloody tough competitor, but it just wasn't the done
thing for a bike racer to cry. But Wayne was always emotional.
He felt deeply about things, he cared about his racing. Perhaps
that's why he went so much further than the other guys he
was racing against at the time—because he cared.'

Willi Praml remembers that Wayne was completely
different from the other riders she and Karl sponsored over the
years. He was deadly serious about his racing, and wanted to
reach the top. 'Wayne used to plaster stickers all over his bike
for spark plugs, oils, helmets or whatever, because he wanted
it to look like he had a lot of sponsorship. Of course he didn't,
and we were trying to get companies to help out. They weren't
interested in putting money into it, because they reckoned they

got the exposure free anyway. We eventually had to ban stickers unless a company was paying for it,' Willi Praml says. 'Wayne was always playing practical jokes on us. He was a cross between Dennis the Menace and a little puppy looking for approval.'

Willi Praml remembers one practical joke Gardner tried to play on a bunch of Launceston schoolgirls. The Praml team was in Tasmania for an Australian title round in 1979, and Gardner and team-mate Wayne Clarke borrowed the hired Pantec truck and headed into town. They saw a crowd of teenage schoolgirls waiting for a bus, and pulled up to offer their services. 'Wayne told the girls the bus company had been hit by a strike back at the depot, and they had been sent in the truck to pick up the passengers,' Willi recalls. 'No-one believed them, and the girls wouldn't get in the truck, but Wayne did manage to let them all know the name of the motel where we were staying and later that night a carload of them came around to pick our boys up. We had a curfew on the boys when preparing for a race, but they just about broke their legs in the rush to climb out the motel window.'

However, Willi Praml did have one moment of triumph against her practical joker rider. It was at Winton, a small track in central Victoria, in 1978 and Gardner was the team's new recruit. 'We were really crowded into a couple of motel rooms, and there wasn't much choice about where everyone would sleep,' Willi says. 'In the end there was one double bed for Wayne and one of the older guys in our team. We wound Wayne up by telling him that the other guy was a bit queer, that he liked teenage boys. Wayne was petrified, and we all fell over laughing when we discovered him in bed for the night dressed in his full racing leather suit, with all the zippers done right up tight!'

As a B-grader, Gardner could compete in Australian title rounds, and in April 1978, armed with a new TZ350, he tackled his first championship event at Oran Park. It was an inauspicious start. Gardner finished tenth behind New Zealander Graeme Crosby, Lee Roebuck, Roger Heyes, Graeme Geddes, Murray Ogilvie, Ron Boulden, Rob Phillis, Andrew Johnson and Gary Coleman. Of the nine, only Crosby made his mark in international racing but, despite finishing second in the 1982 world 500-cc championship, never won a Grand Prix. Gardner remembers being a little over-awed by the company he was keeping, but says he secretly knew he could beat them. 'I knew the time wasn't right to beat those guys, but I never had the slightest doubt I would be better than them, that I would beat the lot of them one day. I didn't speak out loud about it, blow my own bugle, in case it didn't come true, but I always felt I could do better. It was a funny feeling that I had. I don't know why, I just had it. Even today, if some rider does something good and everyone is raving about it, I don't rate it much at all, I just want to go out there and do it better.' Sure enough, Gardner's results started improving and by August 1978 he was promoted to A grade, the youngest ever at just eighteen years and ten months.

Racing in Australia as a privateer was a tough grind, with virtually no sponsorship and hellishly long distances to be travelled for weekend competition. The rewards were almost non-existent, but the effort to compete was considerable. Gardner would spend all week preparing his bike, load it into his utility truck on Thursday night then leave straight from work on Friday afternoon. He'd then drive 1000 kilometres through the night to Queensland, Victoria or South Australia to be ready for practice on Saturday. Often he would sleep in the ute on Saturday night, then drive back to Wollongong after Sunday's racing and front up for work at seven on Monday morning. If the bike needed mechanical attention, he'd find a cheap motel and dismantle the engine in the bathroom, replacing crankshafts or taking apart the motor to clean it up after a piston seizure. The White Horse Inn in Surfers Paradise, Queensland, holds special memories. Its bathrooms saw a number of engine rebuilds over the years, and its towels mopped up plenty of spilt oil and grease.

Facilities at the tracks were never marvellous—be they dusty paddocks at Bathurst and Oran Park or a few square metres of asphalt at Amaroo Park. And it was worse if you'd been driving all Friday night to cover the 1000 kilometres and more from home to an interstate meeting, arriving exhausted on Saturday morning but needing suddenly to switch on and concentrate hard on setting up yourself and the bike for Sunday's racing. Things are different now. Gardner's team mechanics drive to the tracks in a huge transporter equipped as a mobile workshop with every conceivable mechanical aid, his motorhome driver takes the

$300,000s worth of opulence on four wheels and sets it up for him, while the man himself jets in or drives one or another of his luxury cars. The racing is immeasurably harder these days, as is the pressure, but Gardner's physical comfort has long since ceased to be a problem.

By 1979 Gardner was at the forefront of 350-cc-class racing in Australia but had a frustrating year against two better-equipped rivals, Victorian Graeme Geddes and Sydneysider John Pace. Both were fully sponsored and had the latest TZ350 Yamahas with all the performance parts and best tyres. They could pull 240 kilometres per hour down the straight while Wayne would be battling to reach 230. Gardner felt like the poor relation. 'I was straight-out jealous,' he says. 'They both had better bikes and better tyres, and they didn't have to work—they were professional racers. I appreciated what Karl Praml was doing for me but we simply didn't have the budget these guys had. I was really jealous of the deals they had. But what made it worse was that I couldn't beat them, no matter what I did. I tried everything, but they still beat me. If it looked like I would win, the bike would let me down. It would have been easy to blame the machine and say they were better equipped than me, but I started to doubt my ability. Then they both landed deals overseas, and that pissed me off even more. I reckoned I was as good as or better than them, but there was no way I could show what I was capable of.'

By this time Gardner had his first steady girlfriend. He met Donna Forbes at a race meeting at Oran Park in December 1978, when a friend organised a blind date. Donna's first impression was of 'a scruffy little guy with a cold sore on his lip, who was a couple of hours late the first time he took me out'. Donna must have seen more in Wayne than that, because they are still together and Donna has had an enormous input into Gardner's racing career.

CHAPTER 4

'You're Sacked!'

I f everybody's life contains at least one turning point—
a significant event or set of circumstances that
determines success or failure, happiness or tragedy,
and sets a course for the future—then 1980 must go down as
a year-long turning point for Wayne Gardner. He was sacked
from his job, travelled to England and became obsessed with
the idea of becoming the world motorcycle racing champion, won
the biggest race in Australia, and caught the eye of an international
team boss who signed him to ride overseas. Yes, it was a big
year, but it didn't start off too well.

Gardner wasn't exactly a pin-up boy at Tubemakers.
After a weekend's racing interstate, he'd arrive at work on Monday
completely exhausted and looking for somewhere to curl up for
a snooze. Sometimes an obliging workmate would swing him
up by crane to the top of the pile of completed steel pipes. He'd
crawl inside, out of sight, and grab a few hours' sleep. On other
occasions, he wouldn't turn up at work at all. His foreman from
those days, George Denton, remembers that it was a constant
game of cat and mouse trying to catch him sleeping on the job,
with Gardner usually one step ahead. 'I didn't always know where
he was, but he knew exactly where I was all the time,' Denton
remembers. 'He had a lot of hiding places where he'd go for
a sleep. At one stage I couldn't find him anywhere, and eventually
discovered that he was up on the roof. Wayne was a bit of a
lad alright. It was quite clear that he was interested only in
motorbikes, but we tried to keep him out of trouble so that he'd
finish his trade and have something to fall back on if his dream
of becoming a professional motorcycle racer didn't work out.'

Gardner completed his trade—just. The day his
apprenticeship ended Tubemakers sacked him for absenteeism.
'I knew I was in a bit of trouble for missing work, so I tried

to work every day for the last six months of my apprenticeship,'
Gardner recalls. 'An electrical apprentice also had a bad
attendance record and the company decided it didn't want him
when he finished his time. He got the sack but the electricians
said it wasn't fair for him to go if I stayed. They threatened a
big strike to support their man so I was told I'd have to go,
too. Then the fitters said they'd strike on my behalf but I told
them not to bother. I was happy to go.' Despite the circumstance
of Gardner's departure, Denton says the staff at Tubemakers still
take an active interest in his racing career—most sitting up past
midnight on Sundays watching the live telecasts from Europe,
with the race the main topic of conversation in the lunchroom
the next day.

After leaving Tubemakers, Gardner 'bummed around
Wollongong for a while on the dole' before getting casual work
labouring for a bricklayer and behind the spare parts counter
in a motorcycle dealership, Kevin Fraser Motorcycles, which was
also sponsoring him on a TZ350 racer that year. When his
severance pay entitlements from Tubemakers came through,
Gardner decided to spend the lot on a trip to England to study
the standard of the racing scene there. It was a critical career
move, but he was almost too frightened to get on the plane.
'I was just a kid and I was dead scared about the whole trip.
I crashed in a race in Adelaide the Sunday before I was due
to leave, breaking my wrist, and I thought that was a pretty
good excuse to get out of it. But Donna and my parents said
I had to go. I remember sitting at Sydney airport with Donna,
crying my eyes out and saying I didn't want to go. An old man
sitting near us must have had a gutful of this, because he turned
around and got stuck right into me, telling me I should be ashamed
of myself and to stop acting like a baby. I got the shock of my
life, but it had the right effect. I pulled myself together and jumped
on the plane.' Gardner's flight to London went via Tokyo and
Anchorage, Alaska. A homesick Gardner sent Donna his first
postcard from Anchorage.

First stop in Britain was the famed TT Week race meeting
at the Isle of Man. Gardner rubbed shoulders with the cream
of the British riders, and remembers being over-awed when he
met Ron Haslam, then Britain's number one rider. 'I must have

looked a right scrubber, walking around in shorts and T-shirt with rubber thongs on my feet. I cut the plaster off my wrist with a pair of tin snips because I didn't want anyone to think I was a crasher. I thought it was fantastic meeting all the big names. I went drinking with Ron Haslam's manager, Mal Carter of Pharoah Racing, and thought I'd really hit the big time. When I saw Honda Britain's transporter I was sure I wanted to be a factory rider.' Gardner was too frightened to introduce himself to Roger Marshall, another British star. Both Haslam and Marshall were later to become friends and team-mates of Gardner's, and he left them both way behind. But back in June 1980 neither of the two British riders could have imagined the scruffy little Aussie would ever be a threat to them. However, Gardner says he knew he could beat them. 'It's funny, but I saw Ron Haslam ride, and even though I was awestruck meeting him, I knew I could beat him. That little person inside me said I could. It's strange how that little person has always followed me around, all through my career, telling me that I can do it.'

Two Australians, Graeme (Macca) MacGregor and Jeffrey Sayle, were living in England at the time, trying to make a name for themselves as privateers in the cut-throat world of 250-cc Grand Prix racing. They were heading across to Assen in Holland for the Dutch Grand Prix, and invited Gardner along for the ride. Gardner couldn't afford the ferry fare across the English Channel so stowed away in the back of MacGregor's van amidst the bikes, spare tyres and tool boxes. At Assen he helped out preparing MacGregor's bike, and spent the rest of the time drinking in the intoxicating atmosphere of his first Grand Prix. If fate had decreed Gardner should be a Grand Prix racer, it couldn't have picked a better meeting to introduce him to its delights. Assen is probably the greatest Grand Prix of the year, annually attracting huge crowds up to 200,000 in a week-long racing extravaganza. It is about as far removed as the moon from Amaroo Park. In 1980 the huge Dutch crowd went into an absolute frenzy when local hero Jack Middleburg won the 500-cc Grand Prix.

Gardner could hardly believe the colour, glamour and excitement of the Grand Prix circus in full swing, and he took full advantage of the opportunity to meet his heroes, roaming the pits seeking autographs. His biggest hero was American

Taking over Dad's garage (Gardner Collection)

Learning to slide the rear wheel—Lake Illawarra, 1974 (Gardner Collection)

Leader of the pack, aged 14 (Gardner Collection)

First road race—on a 125-cc motocrosser. Oran Park, December 1976 (Gardner Collection)

Wayne's first TZ350 Yamaha (Illawarra Mercury)

Wayne's first big trophy—the Tom Phillis Memorial, June 1979 (Illawarra Mercury)

Heading for a 750-cc class victory in the 1979 Castrol Six-hour on a Z650 Kawasaki (Illawarra Mercury)

Peter Molloy with the bikes Wayne first made his name on—the Mentors Honda Superbike (left) *and the CB1100R production racer* (Illawarra Mercury)

The Wheelie King—Oran Park, September 1980 (Illawarra Mercury)

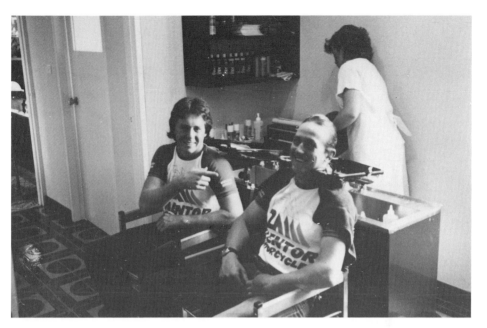

Wayne and Andrew Johnson getting tidied-up for the 1980 Castrol Six-hour, which they won (Billy Hill)

Gardner on his way to victory in the 1980 Castrol Six-hour at Amaroo Park (Illawarra Mercury)

Sweet success for Wayne and Andrew Johnson in the 1980 Six-hour (Illawarra Mercury)

The Moriwaki Kawasaki Superbike—England, 1981 (Gardner Collection)

Getting it up on Moriwaki's Formula One racer—England, 1981 (Gardner Collection)

Gardner leads Barry Sheene (7) and Ron Haslam in an early race in England, 1981 (Gardner Collection)

'I think I need more horsepower—England, 1981 (Gardner Collection)

Just a kid, a long way from home—England, 1981 (Gardner Collection)

Cruising the streets of the old home town (Illawarra Mercury)

'It's not exactly a Ferrari, but we call it home'—Donna and the 'Land Crab' which doubled as a caravan during the English season in 1981 (Gardner Collection)

Celebrating signing with Honda Britain—Cadwell Park, England, 1982 (Gardner Collection)

The magic moment—passing John Pace on the inside with just minutes to go, to win the 1982 Castrol Six-hour at Amaroo (Illawarra Mercury)

Italy's 1982 world 500-cc champion Franco Uncini—badly injured in a crash with Gardner during the Australian's first Grand Prix ride, in Holland, 1983 (Nick Hartgerink)

Home in Australia and heading for victory in the 1984 Swann International Series (Swann Press Picture)

Where are the bikes? Gardner (4th from left) joins the pack for the Le Mans-style start to the 1984 Castrol Six-hour at Oran Park. He finished second (Illawarra Mercury)

There's nothing Wayne can't do on a motorcycle—Wollongong, October 1984 (Illawarra Mercury)

Honda's founder Soichiro Honda, with his latest riding star—Spanish Grand Prix, 1985
(Gardner Collection)

Giving Australian fans a taste of awesome V4 horsepower via a tank-mounted bikecam camera,
Swann Series, Calder Park, November 1985 (Swann Press Picture)

Yamaha ace Kenny Roberts, then well on the way to his third successive world 500-cc championship. After the Dutch Grand Prix, a group of riders, including Roberts, went to Amsterdam to sample the nightlife. Gardner tagged along, and was simply overwhelmed to be in such exalted company. But he made it his business to get as close to Roberts as possible and talk racing as much as he could. It was an experience he will never forget, but the evening also made an impact on Roberts. In his book *Techniques of Motorcycle Racing* (Hazleton Publishing, 1988), Roberts wrote: 'Some guys just race and are happy to say, "Well, I got fifth" or "I got second". Others are different. When I first met Gardner he was little more than a kid, maybe eighteen. [Actually, he was twenty.] He was travelling with Jeff Sayle and had gone to Assen to see what a Grand Prix was all about. We all went to Amsterdam one night, between there and the Belgian Grand Prix, and that's when I met him for the first time. They told me he'd raced in Australia but I didn't know him from Adam. He talked to me quite a bit and he said, "I want to be world champion one day"—and I guess he meant it. Those are the kids who are dangerous, the ones who go to a race and say, "What do I have to do to win that?".'

Gardner also had the chance to do some racing of his own on the six-week trip. A week after the Isle of Man, he went to Donington Circuit and was surprised to discover a bike waiting for him to race. One of Mal Carter's riders, Irishman Donny Robinson, had crashed it the week before and injured himself, so couldn't ride at Donington. Carter had tried all week to contact Gardner and offer him the ride, without success. So when the Australian arrived at the track on the Saturday morning, Carter pointed him at a damaged bike and said, 'Fix that and you can race it tomorrow.' Gardner spent most of the practice sessions working on the bike, a TZ250 Yamaha, so was seriously underprepared for Sunday's race on an unfamiliar track.

'It was a terrible race,' Gardner recalls somewhat ruefully. 'I didn't have a clue about the track or where I was going. I started alright and was keeping up with everyone, but I frightened myself half to death a few times so I slowed right down. I was an accident waiting for a place to happen. And old Mal didn't help. When I was up with the leaders he had a pit board out with a thumbs-up sign. When I started to slow he put out the thumbs-down, then when I dropped right back he put out a sign with a drawing of a snail. It was a really big board, with a huge snail on it. It was bloody embarrassing, and I didn't see the funny side of it at all. I was really mad—going down the straight saying "Fuck you Mal" and giving him the old one-finger sign. I was really hurting, because I had been trying hard to impress him. Once he did that it took all the wind out of my sails.' Gardner eventually finished twelfth, and he returned to the pits to be accosted by an English journalist who told him he was a 'mobile chicane', and not to bother racing in England again. Gardner took special delight in reminding the same journalist of his attack after he became world champion in 1987.

Carter was not impressed by Gardner's efforts. 'After the meeting we all went to the pub at Redgate and I asked Mal how I went. He said he didn't know whether he could offer me a ride, so I suggested I call him when I got back to Australia. He said, "Don't call us, we'll call you" and I was so naive I went back home expecting him to call. I waited and waited, but of course he never rang. Looking back on it, that didn't matter. Going overseas that year and seeing it all, knowing what to expect, and knowing I wanted to be part of it, was probably the most important thing I ever did. I felt I could succeed over there with the right machinery, but most of all I was convinced it was what I had to do. It was the carrot on a stick that drove me from then on.'

If Gardner hadn't exactly made waves in British racing, he was making a bigger splash in a much smaller pond in Australia. But it was on modified, large-capacity streetbikes called Superbikes, not TZ racing machines, that Gardner was making a name for himself with a leading privateer team sponsored by Sydney motorcycle dealers Mentors and radio station 2MMM-FM. Gardner had had his first ride for the team in the 1979 Castrol Six-hour, and they invited him back for a full season in 1980. Ironically, Gardner's arch rival at the time, John Pace, provided both opportunities. The Castrol Six-hour was then Australia's most prestigious production race and Mentors entered a Z650 Kawasaki in the 750-cc class for John Pace and a rider called John Hughes. However, Hughes broke his foot a week before the race and the search was on for a replacement. Pace recommended Gardner to Mentors boss Billy Hill.

Hill says he will never forget his first encounter with Gardner. It was clear from the first time he saw him ride that Gardner had a special talent. 'We had Wayne and another rider in line for the ride, so I went out to Amaroo Park a few days before the race to make the final decision by watching the pair of them go round,' Hill says. 'When I got there Wayne had just crashed the bike. Apparently he had forgotten the gearbox was different from his TZ and had gone up the gearbox the wrong way. The bike was a real mess and we got off to a bad start. But I forgot all that when I saw Wayne ride. It was the moment of truth for him. Here was a nineteen year old with the biggest chance of his career. He'd just thrown the bike down the road and the guy who had to make the decision had arrived to watch him ride. But if he was nervous he didn't show it. He rode so steadily, and with so much conviction in his lines. I still have a clear picture of him coming through one corner on the same line lap after lap. After what he'd gone through it was obvious that here we had something special, so he got the ride.' Pace and Gardner easily won the 750-cc class.

Hill decided to run a Superbike in 1980, and employed noted racing car engineer Peter Molloy to build one based on Honda's CB900, and to run the team. Hill offered the bike to Pace, but he wanted to race in England. Next, Roger Heyes was offered the ride, but at the last moment he sought a release to ride for Honda Australia. Gardner was the third choice, and spent the season riding in baggy leathers made for the much bulkier Heyes, much to his disgust. But it proved third time lucky for the Mentors outfit, and for Gardner, as they successfully took on the might of Honda Australia.

Molloy, who had come from the more refined world of car racing, remembers that his first impressions of Gardner were of 'a rough young larrikin—a little roughneck straight out of the factory'. Gardner credits Molloy with teaching him the meaning of professionalism, of smartening him up and showing him that presentation is half the battle in attracting sponsors and securing good rides. However, Molloy says Gardner was not always a willing pupil.

29

'Wayne was hard to handle, and I found him a bit immature for his age. I'd try to tell him something and he'd say it was all bullshit, that this was bikes, not car racing, and what would I know about it,' Molloy says. 'He desperately wanted to be another Graeme Crosby, doing big wheelstands and that sort of thing. When I first met him he always wanted to play the yahoo, to pull big wheelies and over-impress with his riding, to pat guys on the bum as he passed them. It took me quite a while to get through to him that that wasn't the way to succeed, that you had to concentrate on the race and do the spectacular stuff when it was all over. I told him the big sponsors overseas wouldn't stand for that sort of larrikinism, that they were putting millions of dollars into the sport and they wanted to give the fans someone to look up to. And his presentation was bad. He was quite happy getting around in old shorts and T-shirt. I remember when we went to Daytona in the United States together in 1981. Wayne was invited to go on an interview with American national television and he wanted to turn up in shorts and T-shirt. I told him there was no way, and made him get dressed up. I tried to point out how well the American riders were turned out, with nice clothes and their sponsor's logos on their shirts, nice cars, that sort of thing. It's very important. He realises that now, and his presentation is first class. It wasn't always the case though.

'Having said that, I have never had anything but respect for Wayne as a rider. There was never anything he couldn't ride, and he was very sympathetic to machinery. He never over-revved, and if he did miss a gear or something like that, he'd listen to the engine and make sure it was right before riding hard again. He had all the potential in the world back in 1980. I never had the slightest doubt he would be a world champion. I believed then, and I believe now, that his ability is unmatched by any other rider,' Molloy says. Hill agrees. 'There was never a race that Wayne was riding for me when he didn't do his best, or surpass it,' Hill says.

During 1980 the Mentors team enjoyed great success, at every opportunity tweaking the official Honda Australia team's tail by beating its riders. Gardner won the first two rounds of the nationally televised Bel-Ray Superbike Series at Oran Park to inflict embarrassing defeats on the Honda team. However, his greatest triumph of the year came on 19 October in the Castrol Six-hour race when he teamed with young Victorian hot-shot Andrew Johnson on a Mentors CB1100R Honda. Billy Hill was so convinced his pair would win that he took them to a barber's shop before the race to 'give them both haircuts and smarten them up for the TV presentation afterwards'. Gardner was on the front row of qualifiers, which also qualified him for a television interview before the race. He was tongue-tied and embarrassed, and fluffed his lines. It was another lesson he has never forgotten. Since then he has worked diligently at his presentation and public speaking, and now is at ease on chat shows with some of the biggest television names in the world.

However, Gardner certainly didn't fluff his lines on the track that day. In pouring rain, he completely dominated the event, doing most of the riding and clearing away to a two-lap victory over the Suzuki pairing of old rival John Pace and Neil Chivas, with Honda Australia's Dennis Neill third, a further two laps behind. So convincing was the win that some doubted it was possible. The Suzuki team fired in a protest over alleged lap-scoring irregularities. The matter wasn't resolved for ten months, and then only when Hill took a solicitor, barrister and Queen's Counsel to the Auto Cycle Council of Australia's annual meeting to demand justice—and the prize money.

If the Six-hour fiasco demonstrated how hard teams were prepared to play the game, then the third and final round of the 1980 Bel-Ray Series rammed the point home. Team Honda Australia got its revenge for the hidings it had received at the hands of the Mentors team all season. The race was at Oran Park, in conjunction with a round of the Swann International Series, and Gardner had the title virtually wrapped up. Even if his major rival, Honda's Michael Cole, won the final race, Gardner had only to finish second or third to wrap it up. From the start, Honda's Dennis Neill charged into the lead, followed by Cole, Gardner and Kawasaki's Jim Budd. However, Gardner's Honda started to misfire and he was forced to slow, dropping back to fourth spot. Neill was a long way in front, but on the last lap he slowed dramatically, allowing Cole to catch and pass him to win the series. Gardner, unaware of the trick that the front-runners had conspired to pull on him, thought he had the series won and celebrated with a huge wheelstand across the finishing line. He was devastated when told Cole had won, and Hill was furious. They protested and, although Neill was reprimanded under the rules of racing 'for not making a bona fide attempt to succeed', the result was allowed to stand. 'It taught me never to trust anyone to do the right thing,' Gardner said. Hill says it was an important lesson for the whole team, showing how a large company could react when it was being beaten by its own product. 'I guess they had to justify their budget, and they didn't care how they did it,' he says.

Gardner also entered the Swann Series on a new CB1100R Honda Superbike which Molloy had built. However, his efforts ended when the engine blew up in round two at Surfers Paradise. Meantime, Graeme Crosby had returned from Britain with a Formula One Suzuki and was staging epic dices with Albury rider Steve Trinder, riding an RG500 Suzuki GP machine. A Japanese engineer, Mamoru Moriwaki, was planning to visit Australia for the final Swann round in Melbourne, looking for a good young Australian rider to take to England in 1981. Everyone predicted Trinder would get the ride—until he crashed and broke his leg in the penultimate Swann round in Adelaide. Gardner was sitting at home in Wollongong watching the race on television, and when Trinder crashed he realised he had a chance of catching Moriwaki's eye. 'I rang Molloy straight away and pleaded with him to rebuild the engine so we could go to Sandown in Melbourne for the final race,' he says. Molloy obliged, and the pair went to Melbourne. Once again, fate played its hand.

Superbikes, based as they are on big, heavy four-stroke streetbikes, are no match for purpose-built racing bikes. The racing bikes are more powerful, stop faster and handle better. Their only possible advantage is in rain, when the four-stroke's torque allows a rider to accelerate harder out of corners than his rival on a two-stroke racer with its narrow and peaky power band. Gardner ran his bike in the Swann round for a mid-field placing, then parked it, realising he couldn't hope to match the GP bikes in the final big race of the day, the Australian Unlimited championship. Molloy went up to the control tower to have a beer with race officials, thinking his day's work was over.

However, as the riders were being called for the Unlimited race, it started to rain. Gardner raced to the pits, pulled on his leathers and helmet, and made it to the grid with seconds to spare. When the flag dropped he blasted into the lead and won easily.

The victory had the desired effect on Moriwaki. He was greatly impressed, because a rider who could handle a big four-stroke on wet tracks fitted perfectly into his plans to run a Kawasaki-based Superbike against GP bikes in Britain in 1981. Moriwaki went down into the Sandown pits to seek Gardner out. It's a meeting he still remembers vividly. 'I went down to congratulate him on his ride and to talk about him maybe coming to England with me. I remember looking him in the eye and seeing a special fire there. I thought "One day this boy will be the best rider in the world, he will be world champion for sure." I could see it in his eyes.' Moriwaki still gets animated when he recalls that first meeting with Gardner. The pair struck an immediate rapport, which has strengthened over the years. Gardner still regards the Japanese engineering maestro as a mentor, and turns to him for help and advice often throughout a season. He never goes to Japan's Suzuka Circuit without making a pilgrimage to Moriwaki's home where the pair will sit quietly and dissect his most recent riding performances, searching for improvements. Crosby, who was Moriwaki's partner in marketing the Japanese-made performance parts in Britain, rang Gardner a few weeks after the Swann Series offering him a ride with the team in Britain in 1981. There was no signing on fee, but Gardner would be where he wanted to be—racing overseas on competitive machinery. However, Gardner did not accept straight away. Molloy had put together an attractive deal for the 1981 Australian season, with Gardner being paid $15,000 to ride a Superbike in Australia, with occasional overseas forays. It was a lot of money, and he found it hard to turn down.

CHAPTER 5

'Look Out World, Here I Come'

It takes guts by the truckload to propel a racing motorcycle down a track at 300 kilometres per hour, then grab huge handfuls of brake lever at the end of the straight and maintain control as the bike weaves and shudders, the rear wheel skipping off the ground as the machine protests strenuously at being forced to slow down much too late for the next corner. It takes guts to then twist the throttle as hard as possible and lay a thick line of black rubber out of the corner as the rear wheel spins wildly with 160 horsepower being fed through it onto the tarmac. It takes guts to push yourself through the pain barrier and race a Grand Prix with six broken bones in your foot, and still finish second to stay in the race for the world championship. On the track, Wayne Gardner has guts in abundance. Off the track, though, it's another matter altogether.

Wayne Gardner is soft-hearted—some of his close friends and family say too soft-hearted. Not when preparing for a race, or when he's out on the track. Then his heart turns to stone and his blood to ice. He develops tunnel vision and nothing, and no-one, can distract him from his objective of winning races. However, off the track he's really a softie, although he tries hard not to let any of his rivals know. It doesn't fit the image Gardner likes to portray but perhaps it's what keeps him human in a tough and dangerous sport, where the bottom line is that you risk your life every time you take to the track. He's always been the same. After winning his first big race, the 1980 Castrol Six-hour, he didn't go out celebrating until after he'd driven one and a half hours back to Wollongong Hospital to visit the eleven-year-old son of a Tubemakers workmate who had missed the race because he had just had an appendicitis operation. He finds it hard to say 'no' to requests for his time, although he is becoming tougher on that score as he realises how people have taken advantage of him and his inability to say 'no' in the past. Although Gardner's soft-heartedness has won him a lot of friends, there have been times when it has verged on cowardice and has landed him in trouble . . . for example, when he couldn't tell Peter Molloy he wouldn't be riding for him in 1981.

For all his bravado, Gardner felt somewhat intimidated by Molloy. After winning the Australian title round in the rain at Sandown, Gardner had gone straight to Molloy to shamefacedly apologise for racing the bike without permission. However, his respect for his team boss didn't stop him recognising that he had to accept Moriwaki's offer to go to Britain to further his racing career. The decision hadn't been easy. It was a major step, and Gardner vividly recalls sitting in his car in the driveway of his parents' home, thrashing out the pros and cons with Donna for hours on end. Finally, it was plain there was only one true option—he had to go overseas and race a full season to see if he was good enough to make it in international racing. The only problem was that he couldn't bring himself to tell Molloy. Instead, he allowed Molloy to organise a trip to the biggest meeting of the year in the United States—Daytona Speed Week—early in March 1981. Gardner was to ride a Moriwaki Kawasaki at Daytona and then, or so Molloy thought, return to Australia. Gardner's actual plan was to go on to Britain from the United States. He finally broke the news to Molloy on the plane flight from Sydney.

'Peter was pretty annoyed, and I don't blame him,' Gardner says. 'I really hate letting people down but I had let him down badly. He had gone ahead with the organisation of a team, got the money together and the whole package. There were no bikes yet, but everything else was starting to get rolling. Then of course I pulled the rug out from under him. He tried to tell me not to do it that way, to come back to Australia and we'd do a few trips overseas for major races. But that wasn't for me. I told him that once I went, I wanted to do it properly. All or nothing.' It was a long plane trip.

Molloy may have been disappointed at losing his rider, but he made sure Gardner was fully prepared for his first major race against international stars. 'Peter really pumped me up at Daytona, walking around the pits looking at teams and saying,

"Yeah, we'll beat them, we'll beat them." I met my new Moriwaki team-mate from Britain, Roger Marshall, and he thought I was a right cheeky little upstart, especially when I was with Molloy,' Gardner says. However, once out on the track, Gardner showed he was no upstart, despite never having raced on the famous Daytona speed bowl before, and certainly never having raced against riders of this calibre. Gardner entered the Superbike race and rode superbly for fourth place behind US Suzuki ace Wes Cooley, Graeme Crosby on another Suzuki, and American teenage sensation 'Fast Freddie' Spencer. It was a stunning effort for a novice in top-line competition. Having just beaten a rookie from Downunder out of third place, Spencer was quickly thrust into the 500-cc GP limelight, and two years later was world champion. Gardner, however, didn't have the same connections, and his path to the top was by a much longer, more tortuous route.

Moriwaki hung a 'For Sale' sign on the Superbike in the Daytona pits, because by then he intended Gardner to concentrate on Formula One racing when they got to Britain. Superbikes are basically modified street machines, while Formula Ones are purpose-built, four-stroke racing machines. These days, Superbikes have completely eclipsed F1, but in 1981 in Britain the F1 racing scene was very strong. Moriwaki had decided not to go to the extra expense of campaigning a Superbike in Britain, but changed his mind after he was unable to sell the machine at Daytona. The decision proved of critical importance to Gardner. 'It was the Superbike that made my name in Britain,' Gardner recalls. 'I still rode the F1 bikes hard, but I had most success on the Superbike.' The Superbike hardly looked like a racing bike at all, with its high, wide handlebars that earned it the nickname of the 'sit-up-and-beg bike'. But Gardner could do amazing things on it. In fact, this was how he won his first race of the 1981 British season, beating reigning world F1 champion Crosby, Honda Britain ace Ron Haslam, Moriwaki team-mate Roger Marshall (who rode the F1 machine) and Dave Potter, who rode a potent TZ750 Yamaha GP racer.

The race was at Cadwell Park, Lincolnshire, and Gardner says he had Marshall to thank for the win. 'When I arrived in Britain from Daytona I caught a train up to Lincolnshire and stayed with Roger. Cadwell Park wasn't far from his home, and most days he would take me over to the track in his Ford Granada and drive me around the circuit, showing me the racing lines and so on. By the time the race came around I knew it pretty well,' Gardner says. 'It was a bit embarrassing though. During practice I was faster than Roger, and Moriwaki kept my times a secret so as not to upset Roger.' When the racing started Gardner got away in sixth place, but he quickly made his way through the field, until, much to his surprise, he found himself closing rapidly on race leader Crosby, on his works Suzuki.

'Croz owned half of Moriwaki UK, so in effect he was actually my boss, and I didn't really want to overtake him in my first race. I was happy with the idea of coming second but Croz was actually holding me up and I could see Dave Potter was closing in on both of us. I remember thinking "Hurry up Croz, hurry up", then I decided to pass him to stir him up and make him go faster and pass me back. But once I got in front I realised Croz couldn't pass me back so I just put my head down and went for it. Dave Potter caught us on the last lap and the three of us went over the line virtually locked together. But I had won, and I couldn't believe it. I thought Croz may have been really mad with me, but he was great, and Moriwaki was so, so happy.'

If the first-up victory shocked Gardner, it surprised Marshall even more. He had gone into the race as number-one rider in the Moriwaki outfit, but had been relegated to number two in no uncertain manner. Although it must have been a cruel blow to his pride, Marshall never allowed it to affect his friendship with the young Aussie, and the two have remained staunch friends ever since they first teamed up. Marshall recalls that his first thoughts after that Cadwell Park race were that Gardner would one day become world champion. 'He just blitzed the lot of us. Hell, that was my home track and I had raced there hundreds of times and I couldn't even get close.'

If Gardner was showing great confidence on the track, off it he was a lonely and homesick Wollongong kid. Within a week of arriving in Britain he had phoned home to his girlfriend, Donna Forbes, and 'on the spur of the moment', begged her to fly over and join him in Britain. Donna was seventeen at the time, but didn't hesitate. And her parents raised no serious objections to their daughter flying to the other side of the world to join her penniless boyfriend who was trying to make it as a professional motorcycle racer. 'Dad had a few reservations— I guess he thought I was a bit young. But Mum was confident that I knew what I was doing and they even paid my airfare. It was a day I'll never forget,' Donna recalls.

Gardner's inability to last a week alone in Britain demonstrates a basic insecurity that he readily admits. It is something that hasn't changed over the years, despite his success. 'I'm certainly not a loner, I know that. I need people around me all the time—people I know and can trust, people I can be myself with,' he says. Gardner is wary of latecomers trying to hitch a ride on his fame and fortune. Apart from Donna, his most constant companions are Wilf Needham, a laconic Londoner who has been one of his mechanics since 1982, and Harris Barnett, his manager since late 1981, who fusses over Gardner to his constant amusement and eternal gratitude.

Donna arrived in Britain in time to see Wayne win that first race at Cadwell Park and 1700 pounds (3400 dollars) in prize money. They used the money to buy an old Austin 1800 (dubbed 'the Land Crab'). It was their transport for the year and, more often than not, a place to sleep at the racetracks because they didn't have enough spare cash for hotel rooms.

Two weeks after his win at Cadwell Park, Gardner lined up at Donington, scene of his embarrassing debut the year before. This time, though, he wasn't in some minor 350-cc support race, but the main event—against the top American riders. Gardner was overwhelmed to be in the field, and even more so when he qualified on the front row of the grid. 'There was Kenny Roberts on his Yamaha, and Randy Mamola on a Suzuki—all the greats, and there I was on the front row of the grid. I said to Donna, "Whatever you do, get a photo of me on the grid with all these flash guns". I finished fifth or sixth, but I didn't care. I had been on the front row with Kenny Roberts and I was rapt.' Gardner also contested the Motorcycle News Superbike race, holding out until the last lap against British legend and two-times world 500-cc champion Barry Sheene, on a TZ500 Yamaha GP bike. 'I was too scared to beat him,' Gardner says of that race.

Sheene was impressed, writing later in his column in

British Motorcycle News, 'What a fantastic rider Wayne Gardner is. Without doubt, he's the best braker I have come up against. During the MCN Superbike race at Donington he outbraked me every time coming into Park Corner at the end of the fast Starkeys Straight. And every time I thought "He's never going to stop that great four-stroke", but he did. There was no suggestion of wild riding. He simply knows what he's doing with that big Moriwaki. I'm not noted for being an early braker into corners, but I had the rear wheel of my Yamaha off the ground a couple of times trying to outdo him. In the end I took a deep breath and just managed to get inside him as we went around Redgate for the last time, and I had to work all the way to beat him by a few yards.'

Gardner was enjoying the lessons he was learning in the tough school of English short-circuit racing. 'The tracks were much faster than I was used to at home and that took a while to adjust to, but I really enjoyed the racing. The English lads were very competitive and I always knew I'd been in a race. Then from time to time GP riders such as Sheene would come home for a meeting and that was the chance to gauge what progress I was making. I was enjoying the life of a full-time professional—only having to worry about the bikes and my riding, not having a job to go home to after each meeting. And, of course, the distances we had to travel to race were so much shorter than in Australia. No more 1000-kilometre overnighters.'

In 1981, after staying with Roger Marshall in the first months, Wayne and Donna found a flat in one of Britain's less salubrious locations—Coalville, Leicestershire. A year later they bought a house in Wragby, a pleasant little village on the wide, open grainfields of Lincolnshire. Wragby was virtually surrounded by all of England's major racetracks. Cadwell Park was just fifteen minutes' drive away, Donington an hour, and Oulten, Snetterton, Scarborough and Silverstone all an hour and a half.

Of the British tracks, Oulten was Gardner's favourite. 'It was a nice track, a real classic circuit with a feeling of history and an interesting layout with lots of ups and downs. I also liked Donington, which is quite fast, and Silverstone. But the one I hated was Scarborough, up in the north-east of England.

It had been converted from an old bicycle racing track and was very narrow and dangerous. It seemed like someone got killed there at least once a year and I hated racing on it. Eventually I refused to.' Gardner also refused to ride on the Isle of Man, whose notorious road circuit has also claimed many lives over the years. The circuit is steeped in history and is dear to the hearts of all British motorcycle racing fans, who have lamented its decline in status since it was stripped of a round of the world 500-cc championship in the mid-1970s. Apart from traffic, the track has everything that a normal road rider must contend with: lampposts, manhole covers, kerbs and gutters, stone walls and fences—even the occasional sheep or cow. Yet the racing speeds approach 300 kilometres per hour. When Gardner refused to race there, he earned the ire of many British fans and criticism from the British motorcycle press. 'I've been called everything from a poser to a coward for not racing there, but there was no way. I went there as a spectator a couple of times and that was enough for me. It's got nothing to do with courage—I certainly don't think I have to prove that. It's simply a cold, hard professional decision not to expose yourself to risk on a dangerous track. Injuries can happen anywhere, at any time, but there is no sense in unnecessarily exposing yourself to risks.'

At the end of May, Gardner crashed and fractured his ankle, which should have put his racing on hold for a month or two. He had been entered in his first race in Japan, the Suzuka 200- kilometre, but that seemed to be out of the question. 'Donna and I went over to the Isle of Man to watch the races there at the beginning of June, but I really wanted to go to Japan. I thought "What the hell", soaked the plaster cast off my ankle, caught a light plane to London, flew to Japan and won the race— to Moriwaki's great delight.' The victory brought Moriwaki's small company great publicity and prestige in his home market.

Gardner may have had some success, but he was still nothing more than a spectator in the big world of Grand Prix bike racing—and a budget-priced spectator at that. He and Donna managed to cadge a lift to the Belgian Grand Prix at the Francorchamps Circuit near Spa by offering to drive a car owned by Ruth Randle, who was sponsoring the 250-cc racing effort of fellow Australian Jeff Sayle. They slept in the car in the carpark of Randle's hotel, and for breakfast and lunch ate bread rolls smuggled out from the hotel dining-room. They did manage to get into the pits at Spa, and Gardner remembers wandering around looking at the teams' transporters and riders' motorhomes and feeling it was another world, one to which he desperately wanted to belong. When he and Donna went to the Austrian Grand Prix at the spectacular Salzburgring, they watched the action from the hillside with 80,000 fanatical Austrians and Germans. 'I can never go to the Salzburgring without looking up at that hillside and remembering sitting up there watching my idols like Kenny Roberts and dreaming of one day being part of it. It is quite an emotional thing for me—it reminds me where I've come from,' Gardner says.

If Gardner was still only dreaming of making it to the top, others had more concrete plans for him. The English team bosses had noted his progress with interest during the season, and all felt he had what it took. In the pits at Spa during the Belgian Grand Prix, the bosses of Britain's three biggest race teams all approached him within minutes of each other, offering rides for 1982. 'Barry Symmonds from Honda Britain bumped into me in the pits and told me not to do anything about the next year until I had spoken to him. I was still getting over the shock when Martin Ogborne from Suzuki came up and told me he had seen Barry talking to me, and I shouldn't make any decision to sign with Honda until I had spoken to him. Then the Yamaha guys came up to me with an offer as well. I couldn't believe it.' Gardner may have been surprised to get three offers, but he quickly turned the situation to his advantage, stretching Symmonds from his original offer of 15,000 pounds to a 27,000-pound signing-on fee. 'I was pretty pleased with that,' Gardner recalls with some satisfaction. 'It was my first real attempt at negotiating and it was quite good money for what I was doing at the time.'

Gardner was signed to ride Honda's 1000-cc works Formula One racers—big, powerful four-strokes. It wasn't a Grand Prix ride but at least it was factory machinery, and Gardner was delighted. He felt he was getting somewhere with his racing. But the news didn't please everyone. When it leaked out at an end-of-year meeting at Brands Hatch, Gardner came in for some vitriolic criticism from an unexpected quarter. Jeffrey Sayle, who despite his talent had struggled for success and recognition as a privateer 250-cc GP rider, was scathing of his fellow Australian's decision to sign with the semi-works Honda Britain team to race four-strokes. Sayle considered Gardner had taken an easy option, and told him so. 'Jeffrey had a real go at me, saying I was taking the easy way out by not racing in GPs, and by staying in Britain and so on. He accused me of trying to get into a factory GP team by the back-door, which I agree I was trying to do—I wasn't trying to hide it. He made me feel really small and embarrassed in front of everyone there at the time—Ruth Randle and all the crew. In a way he made me question what I was doing, but I thought "Stuff him, I'll do it my way. He's only jealous because I'm getting paid and he's not." He was just living from week to week doing Grand Prix racing. I decided I wasn't going Grand Prix racing until I could do it properly. I wasn't going to go busting my gut like he was, and getting nothing for it. That was a road leading to nowhere, and I didn't want that. I wanted to get my foot in the back door with Honda.'

At the end of the 1981 season Gardner gave Moriwaki a farewell gift by returning to Australia and winning the Swann Insurance International Series. He also gave some poor, unfortunate Briton and London's Hilton Hotel unwelcome parting gifts. 'When I bought my car, the Land Crab, I never bothered to have the registration papers changed over to my name. I didn't care much what I did in it, and used to park it anywhere I wanted, so pretty soon I had a glove box full of parking tickets made out to the previous owner. By the time we were ready to go home to Australia at the end of 1981, the car was on its last legs, so I planned to drive it to Heathrow Airport and simply leave it in the carpark. But I couldn't find the airport, and I was starting to worry about missing the plane when I spotted the Hilton Hotel. I drove the old wreck straight into the driveway and Donna and I grabbed our bags, threw the keys at the doorman, jumped into the nearest taxi and made a fast getaway to the airport.' Gardner still can't retell the story without laughing uproariously. The larrikin from Wollongong was still alive and well despite a year overseas.

Wayne Gardner (left) *and his friend Barry Sisson, with the bike they found on a factory rubbish pile* (Gardner Collection)

Gardner aboard the big Moriwaki Kawasaki at Scarborough in England, 1981 (Gardner Collection)

Riding the Honda Britain 1000-cc Formula One machine at Donington Park, England, 1982 (Gardner Collection)

A full-time Grand Prix racer at last—Austrian Grand Prix, Salzburg, 1985 (Rothmans Press Service)

CHAPTER 6

Money, Money, Money

Money, not just dreams of Grand Prix glory, motivated Gardner in his early years with Honda Britain. He would scour the race programmes before each meeting, not to check the calibre of his opposition but to see what prize money was being offered. These days, money is about the last thing Gardner needs to worry about. Careful planning and investments, as well as lucrative endorsements, should guarantee him much more than mere financial security. But things were different in the early years in Britain. When Gardner earned 1700 pounds for his first win at Cadwell Park in 1981, the money was immediately accounted for by buying the Land Crab and setting aside meagre living expenses for Donna and himself for the indeterminate future. They spent the first few months lodging with Roger Marshall before moving into a small flat. The doyen of international motorcycle photographers, veteran Don Morley, likes to recount stories of taking Gardner out 'for a jolly good feed' because he was worried the young Australian wasn't eating properly during those early days in England.

'In 1981 all I was worried about was results, and getting noticed, but in 1982 and 1983, and probably into 1984, all I cared about was money,' Gardner recalls. 'That was my motivation for racing. You could pick up 500 or 1000 pounds for most of the races in Britain and before each meeting I would look in the programmes and see what the prize money was for first place. I was money hungry, it was as simple as that. I wasn't so much concerned about the results, just the money. I used to look at the big-name guys at the time who were probably earning two or three hundred thousand dollars and think "Wow, that's fantastic", and I loved their big motorhomes. Of course I realised that, if the results came, so would the money, but it was the money I was interested in. Then, by the end of 1984, my attitude completely changed. I guess I had enough money in the bank by then not to have to worry about it, and I could concentrate solely on the results.'

At the end of 1981, when Gardner signed with Honda Britain for the next season, Barry Symmonds did him a bigger favour than merely providing him with a job. Symmonds, who had seen a number of his riders get horribly tangled up with taxation problems, advised Gardner to seek professional help. Symmonds recommended Harris Barnett, a qualified accountant and lawyer who had worked with sportsmen at Mark McCormack's International Management Group in London before going out on his own. Gardner dropped in to Barnett's office on the way to the airport during the Land Crab's infamous last journey.

'Harris started talking about companies and how we'd have to do this and do that, and I didn't understand a word he was talking about,' Gardner says. 'We were in his office in Mayfair, in the hoity-toity part of London, and I was a bit lost by it all. Harris said he'd need 2000 pounds to set up the business. That was all I had on me and I needed 600 to pay for my plane ticket home. I pulled out all the money, threw it on the table, counted out 600 and told him to have the rest and I'd send him the balance when I got home to Australia. I was so naive, I didn't even ask for a receipt. When I got home I asked my Mum to lend me $1000 to send over to this little Pakistani I'd met who was going to look after my money. Poor Mum didn't know what to think, but she lent me the money, and Harris and I haven't looked back.

'In fact, my relationship with Harris has worked out perfectly. We are more like father and son or brothers than business partners. He's a person I can trust, and that's very important. I can't concentrate on racing while watching all my business affairs. It's impossible. You've got to trust somebody and I trust Harris one hundred per cent.'

As it happens, Harris Barnett is about as far removed from being a Pakistani as is possible. He is a South African Jew, and he chuckled when he found out years later that he had been mistaken for a Pakistani. He also laughs at the memory of

Gardner's obvious confusion in his office the first time they met. 'I wondered what on earth we had here—a young Australian who dumped some cash on my desk, then raced out to catch a plane home to Australia saying he'd send me the rest,' Barnett recalls. 'I didn't know what would come of it, or whether I could ever expect to see the rest of the money or him again. But sure enough, a cheque arrived a week later and we were in business.' They were an unlikely partnership, the rough and ready young Australian racer and the worldly wise London businessman twenty years his senior, but since then they have developed a close and highly effective business relationship, and an even closer friendship.

Gardner thought he had pulled the right rein joining Honda Britain for the 1982 season. After all, Honda was the biggest motorcycle manufacturer in the world and had the biggest team in British racing. Surely it would have the best bikes as well. However, it didn't quite work as planned. Roger Marshall had taken the ride Gardner rejected with the Suzuki team, and was about to turn the tables on Gardner from the previous season. Marshall won the TT Formula One and Superbike titles in a crushing blow for Honda. 'Roger had his best year ever in 1982,' Gardner recalls. 'The package was a good one—a very competitive bike and a strong rider. I couldn't often beat him but I wasn't overly worried because I knew my team-mate Ron Haslam was moving on to Honda's Grand Prix team and I already had a contract for the 1983 season. I thought I'd be Honda Britain's number one, and the bikes would be better the next year.'

He was in for a rude shock. Honda signed Marshall for 1983, and Gardner felt very much as if he had been shunted sideways. 'I was pissed off. One moment I was Honda Britain's number-one rider and the next I wasn't any more. Roger had come into the team having won the titles, so he was obviously number one. I wasn't happy. In fact, I remember a publicity photo of me and Roger where I couldn't raise a smile at all—I was so angry because Roger was sitting on my bike and I was pushed away in the corner.' The experience was repeated in October 1988 when Eddie Lawson joined the Rothmans Honda team after his surprise defection from Yamaha; and it didn't feel any better the second time around.

The 1982 season hadn't been a complete wipe-out for Gardner. He shared the British Streetbike championship with Haslam when both rode the very potent CB1100R Hondas, and in one sensational four-week period in June/July he won the Penang Grand Prix, successfully defended his Suzuka 200 crown in Japan, then took out his first race on European soil—the Portuguese round of the world Formula One championship at Vila Real in Portugal. Back home in Australia at the end of the season in October, he showed all the benefits of his overseas experience with a masterful display in the Castrol Six-hour race at Amaroo Park.

Billy Hill from Mentors sponsored Gardner in the Six-hour, and he still believes the race was Gardner's finest, despite his considerable Grand Prix successes in the years since. Gardner's team-mate, fellow Wollongong rider Wayne Clarke, started the race but glazed the tyres on their CB1100R and slipped from first to twenty-fifth, one and a half laps behind the leaders. Gardner pulled back the deficit, then had to repeat the effort later in the race when a slow wheel change cost the team dearly. In an enthralling final hour, Gardner stalked race leader John Pace on an identical machine, clawing back his lead before sweeping to the front with less than ten minutes to go. 'It was something I'll never forget as long as I live,' Hill enthuses. 'The way Wayne carved through the traffic on that tight track was simply sensational. With an hour to go he was back in tenth place but we knew he could win it. I have never seen a better ride, by Wayne or anybody else. And one thing that stuck out above all else was when Wayne saved a huge slide, when the bike tried to high-side him. He never missed a beat and in fact set a lap record the very next lap.'

At the end of 1982 Honda took Gardner to Malaysia for the Selangor Grand Prix to introduce him to the delights of 500-cc Grand Prix motorcycles—in this case Honda's V3 RS500, which Honda Britain would be racing in 1983. Gardner had never raced a 500 before and was immediately impressed by how light and powerful the bike was, and how well it handled. However, that's not the reason he remembers that first race experience of a 500. The race was run in two heats and, after coming second in the first, Gardner crashed in the second. He still winces at the memory. 'I crashed and took this great hunk of meat out of my hand,' he says, indicating a large red scar on the palm of his hand. 'They didn't really clean out all the dirt and by the time I got home to Australia it was all infected. I had to go to hospital because it was down to the bone, and they scraped out all the muck with a toothbrush. I was crawling on the ceiling with the pain.'

Gardner returned to Britain for the 1983 season, determined to beat Roger Marshall. 'I bit my tongue about Roger joining the team because, apart from anything else, he was a good friend and I didn't want any trouble between us. But when it came to racing, I really lashed out. It fired me up just like the Eddie Lawson thing had.'

However, Gardner's zeal and enthusiasm suffered an embarrassing setback in the first minute he was back on an English track. Barry Symmonds took the new RS500s to Brands Hatch on a chilly March morning for the team's first test session. The team was planning to use Dunlop tyres but the tyre technicians hadn't arrived with the stock, so Gardner decided to do a few laps on the standard Michelins already fitted. He headed out of pit lane and around a couple of corners before disaster struck at the first left-hand corner. 'I just fell off,' he remembers, 'because the tyres were new and cold. There was no other explanation because I was only doing about three miles an hour. I couldn't believe it. I just watched the bike go down the hill and hit the wall, and it smashed everything—the seat, the tank—the exhaust pipes were bent over backwards and the chassis was bent. What a mess it made.

'I was so embarrassed, and I can remember thinking "What'll I do? I can't go back and face the team in the pits." I decided to run away. I remember walking towards the fence and looking for a gate to get through. I just didn't want to go back and face the rest of the guys back in the pits. It was the worst I'd ever felt—writing off a brand-new RS500. Symmonds couldn't believe it—our brand-new 500 wrecked in two corners. And the worst thing about it was that the Dunlop tyre truck turned up a few minutes later. The Dunlop guys really paid me out.'

Despite the initial setback, Gardner quickly came to

terms with the demands of racing a GP bike and dominated the British Motorcycle News Masters and Shell Oils 500-cc titles. He was also dominating the Formula One scene on his 850-cc Honda. So, when the team headed to Holland for the Dutch GP meeting at the end of June to contest an F1 support event, Symmonds decided to reward Gardner for his efforts. Symmonds took Gardner's RS500 along and entered him in his first world championship Grand Prix. However, what should have been the greatest moment of his career to date ended in disaster—and almost death—after little more than one lap.

CHAPTER 7

A Deadly Profession

Death stalks the Grand Prix motorcycle circus. It's not up front, not out in the open. It's not often talked about, but it's always there. Although they try to ignore it, and dislike any hint of media sensationalism, all the riders know theirs is a dangerous sport. They all know other competitors who have died in racetrack crashes. Some have been close friends and their loss has been keenly felt. One top 500-cc Grand Prix rider, Ron Haslam, has lost two brothers on the track. Put simply, you can't race a motorcycle at speeds up to 300 kilometres per hour and expect no element of danger. Perhaps that's why there is a certain camaraderie amongst even the strongest rivals, and why the riders live life to the full away from the track.

Gardner has come face to face with death on the racetrack twice in his career. In 1982 English rider John Newbold crashed in front of him while the pair were dicing for third place in a race on the Ulster street circuit. Newbold smashed his head on the kerbing and died soon afterwards. It was a deep shock for the young Australian, who promised Newbold's widow he would never race at the circuit again. But nothing could prepare Gardner for the impact of his other brush with death—at the 1983 Dutch Grand Prix.

Lining up on the grid with all his heroes in front of 150,000 people at arguably the world's greatest motorcycle meeting should have been the greatest moment of Gardner's career, the culmination of all his dreams. At Assen the 6.2-kilometre circuit is surrounded by earthen embankments where the fans line up twenty deep. It gives the circuit a marvellous amphitheatre atmosphere which is enjoyed by riders and spectators alike.

Things started well enough in the 1983 Dutch GP at

Assen, with Gardner qualifying in the top ten despite the fact that his production RS500 Honda was considerably down on power compared to the works Yamahas, Hondas and Suzukis. The unknown Aussie on the third row of the grid was barely noticed, but he was about to have a far greater impact on the race than he ever could have imagined, and certainly much greater than he ever could have wanted. When the field blasted off Gardner found himself up with the leaders, in sixth place in a tightly bunched pack. However, as the riders passed the start line for the first time, Kenny Roberts and the reigning world champion, Italian Franco Uncini, rocketed past him using the power of their works machines to telling effect.

Disaster struck soon afterwards. The rear wheel of Uncini's Suzuki slid sideways, bit into the bitumen then twisted the bike violently in the opposite direction, flinging the little Italian over the handlebars. He landed in the middle of the track, with twenty-five racing bikes screaming towards him at high speed. His training should have told him to stay where he was and allow the other riders time to see him and take evasive action. However, dazed and confused, Uncini made a crouching run for the side of the track—on a collision course with Wayne Gardner.

The impact was sickening. The right handlebar of Gardner's Honda caught Uncini flush on the side of the helmet, ripping it from his head and sending his body cart-wheeling down the track. Gardner slewed off the side of the track, was thrown over the handlebars and landed in a drainage ditch. Back in the pits, Donna was frantic. The Dutch commentator on the public address system was screaming about the accident, but the only words Donna could understand were the names *Uncini* and *Gardner*. She knew something was terribly wrong but no-one would tell her what the commentator was saying. 'They didn't want to alarm me, but it only made it worse,' Donna recalls. 'I was out of my mind with worry and all I could do was run to where I thought the accident had happened, but I got to a gate and wasn't allowed through.' Perhaps it was as well that she couldn't reach the accident location. There she would have found a scene of horrific proportions.

Ambulancemen were tending the two riders, but it was Uncini who was causing most concern. He was gravely ill, with terrible injuries including a fractured skull, broken nose and broken ribs. He was unconscious, and being loaded gingerly into an ambulance for the journey to hospital. There wasn't much hope that he would survive. Gardner had escaped lightly by comparison, with a broken knuckle on his right hand where the handlebar had collided with Uncini's helmet and a few bumps and bruises. Physically he was okay. Mentally, he was deeply hurt even though he couldn't have avoided the accident. After treatment, Gardner returned to the near-deserted pits to find Donna. 'He came up to me and I was crying,' Donna remembers. 'Wayne said, "I'm alright, don't cry" then put his head on my shoulder and howled. We just stood there in the middle of the pits crying, not caring what anyone thought.'

When they had recovered their composure, the pair went to the bar in the pits at Assen to seek out their Australian friends. Gardner's injured knuckle was wrapped in a tea-towel full of ice. The reception they got was unexpected, and upsetting. 'Jeff Sayle told me I got what I deserved—that I wasn't good enough to be out there with those riders and the accident shouldn't have happened,' Gardner says. Donna remembers Wayne sitting slumped on a chair, in pain and still shocked by the accident. 'The others were paying out on him. It wasn't fair. He was upset enough without that,' she says.

Gardner's hurt deepened when he and Donna went to Groningen University Hospital later that evening to check Uncini's progress. They were confronted in the hospital waiting room by members of Uncini's team, and the volatile Italians let Gardner know they considered him fully responsible for the condition of their world champion rider. Gardner tried to explain what had happened to team boss Roberta Gallina. 'He just kept saying, "My Franco, he never crash. My Franco, he never crash." He simply didn't believe that it could have been Franco's fault. He just looked at me as a guy in my first Grand Prix, and his rider as world champion, and decided it had to be my fault. I knew there wasn't anything else I could have done, but it didn't make it any easier. I felt absolutely terrible. It was the worst day of my life,' Gardner says. Donna says she will never forget the look of hatred in Gallina's wife's eyes when they entered the hospital.

51

'When I finally got to see Franco, it was even worse. I couldn't believe what I saw. He was just lying there with tubes and wires attached all over him—just lying there twitching. To make matters worse, Franco had been quite a good friend. I had met him a year before and we had hit it off really well. He might have been the world champion but he was one of the few top riders who could even be bothered to talk to a starry-eyed kid like me. I couldn't believe that I had done this to another human being, let alone Franco. All I could think of was, if this was motorcycle racing, I didn't need it. I wanted to pull out then and there, retire, go home to Wollongong and forget all about racing motorcycles. If Franco had died, I would have stopped racing.'

Fortunately for all concerned, that didn't happen. Uncini came out of his coma within a week and began a slow path to a full recovery. He even returned to the racetrack a year later, although he never regained his world-championship winning ability. Gardner returned to Britain after the crash deeply depressed and uncertain about his racing future. There was a major British meeting a fortnight later, and Gardner didn't want to race. But his close friend and Honda Britain team-mate Roger Marshall would have nothing of it. 'Roger could see how depressed I was, so he was at me all the time, telling me the Assen accident wasn't my fault, that it just couldn't be avoided. He just wouldn't hear of me tossing it in and going home, and in the end I pulled myself together,' Gardner says. In fact, he did more than that, winning his next race, the ITV World of Sport International at Donington Park, where he came from tenth to hit the lead in the final few laps.

Gardner looks back on the Uncini crash as one of the critical points in his career. 'It was hugely important to me,' he says. 'At the time I thought it was the end of the world, but fortunately Franco pulled through. It taught me a lot about racing and the dangers. I had been too blasé before that. I didn't respect the element of danger enough. That crash changed everything. I started to think much more deeply about safety, and how to ride safely but quickly. Of course racing has some danger—it would be foolish to say it hasn't. What is important is respecting that and riding accordingly.

'I've always got butterflies in my stomach before a race. I'm always scared. I suppose you'd say you need guts to ride these bikes. You've got to be brave to be racing at 300 kilometres per hour on a motorcycle along a thin strip of bitumen, but you've also got to be afraid as well. Maybe my limits are higher, but I've still got the fear and respect of danger. Maybe I can ride within those limits longer than most, but I have that fear every time I got out to race. If I didn't have that fear, I'd be worried. If I wasn't afraid of the consequences when I went out to race, then I'd give up—because I'd probably kill myself. Fear makes you concentrate harder than anything else.'

Gardner says he is usually riding at ninety per cent of his ability. 'You simply can't ride at 100 per cent all the time. You can only do that in short bursts, when you really need to. Usually my race lap times are a second or so off what I did in qualifying, when I was pushing it to 100 per cent for a good grid position, so there is a margin there for safety. And I trust most of the other riders not to do anything stupid. They all respect the speed and the danger to each other's lives. Occasionally [French rider] Christian Sarron might rush up the inside, braking for a corner, something stupid like that, trying to prove something, but basically they are all pretty good.'

After crashing at his first GP, Gardner rode fifty-two more before he crashed again, and once again it was not his fault. His engine seized in the Austrian Grand Prix of 1988 as he and Eddie Lawson were dicing for the lead midway through the race. However, Gardner has lost count of the times he has crashed during GP qualifying sessions and testing. 'You use the qualifying sessions before a GP to define the limits of yourself and your bike,' he says. 'Obviously you don't want to fall off during the race but you want to go as fast as possible. So you push and push in practice, and sometimes you push too hard and fall off. Then you know not to push that hard during the race.

'Sometimes I'm just like a little boy who plays with fire knowing he's going to burn himself and pushing it until he does. I'm like that at times when I'm practising. I'll push it and push it on a particular corner, and then I'll fall off and wonder why.' Gardner says crashing is an unusual sensation. 'First you think

"Oh shit, what have I done here?" The next thought is to get well clear of the bike so it doesn't hit you as you slide along, then you look for obstacles you don't want to hit, and you try to avoid them. But your mind is still travelling at 250 kilometres per hour, or whatever, so your reactions are instant. Most riders tend to fall off more when they are starting out, because they haven't learnt their limits yet and probably because they haven't got all the skills yet. You get plenty of practice at falling off.'

Gardner certainly got plenty of practice at the not-so-gentle art of crashing motorcycles during 1983. After the Uncini accident, followed by the Brands Hatch victory, the season turned decidedly sour for him. He entered the British Grand Prix at Silverstone and qualified ninth on his RS500, the first non-works bike on the grid, but a twisted crank ruined his race effort and he limped home in sixteenth place. To further jolt his already shaky confidence, two Suzuki riders, Peter Huber (Sweden) and Norman Brown (Britain), died when they collided in a fifth-lap crash that saw the race halted and restarted.

The only bright spot on an otherwise bleak afternoon at Silverstone was Gardner's victory on his 850-cc four-stroke in the TT F1 race, which clinched the British title with two rounds to go. However, Gardner didn't glean much satisfaction from that victory. As far as he was concerned, the only race that mattered was the GP. He felt that he had blown his chance to show the racing world that the Uncini crash was an aberration, that he really could ride a 500-cc GP motorcycle. As he said at the time, 'It [the TT title] was a bit like winning $5000 in the lottery when your ticket is one off half a million dollars.'

From there, everything went downhill. Gardner crashed while practising at Donington in September, breaking two fingers and cracking his collarbone. Consequently, he was in some pain when he returned to Australia in October to defend his Castrol Six-hour crown for the Mentors team. Disaster struck during practice, when he crashed at 150 kilometres per hour. 'I had a real BIG one,' Gardner admits ruefully, pointing to a scar the size of a saucer on his right shoulder. 'That's what that scar's from. I must have slid about 200 metres, and I woke up in gah-gah land. I didn't know what had happened.' Reluctantly, Gardner pulled out of the race and limped back to Britain sporting two broken knuckles and minus a lot of skin.

He had just one meeting to get through in Britain, at Brands Hatch. All he had to do was finish moderately well in three races, and he would wrap up the Shellsport 500 and the Masters and British 500-cc championships to add to the TT F1 title he had picked up earlier in the season. But, to use racing jargon, he lucked out. 'In the first race, a British rider called Graham Wood crashed right in front of me. I had to run wide onto the grass to avoid him and ended up slamming into a concrete wall. They thought I'd broken my hip,' Gardner recalls. 'I had to go to hospital and I was a right mess—mentally as well as physically. My hip wasn't broken but I was badly knocked around. I was hurting mentally too. I'd lost the three championships because of one guy, in one race.'

Gardner spent the next few weeks recuperating in Harris Barnett's London home. A bed had to be brought downstairs because he could hardly move, and Gardner had plenty of time to reflect on where his sport was leading him. 'I thought "Stuff this! What am I doing this for? This is bullshit. I'm giving this racing a miss, I'm going home." I had no confidence, and had really started questioning myself about whether I had the ability to get anywhere, whether it was worth taking the risk of really smashing myself about.

'I was a mess. Donna was home in Wollongong and I rang her and was bawling my eyes out. My Dad got on the phone and told me to give it a miss, to come home and forget about racing. It was terrible—everything just fell to pieces. There was no GP ride for the next year, and I felt like I hadn't achieved anything.'

Gardner returned home to Wollongong for the Australian summer, and seriously contemplated giving up racing. However, unwittingly, Britain's motorcycle racing fans saved Gardner's career by voting him Man of the Year in a reader's poll conducted by Britain's leading motorcycle magazine, *British Motorcycle News*. He had beaten all the world's best GP riders, including England's favourite sons Barry Sheene and Ron Haslam, in the poll, to join some of the greats of the past, including world champions Mike Hailwood, Giacomo Agostini, Phil Read and John Surtees.

'That lifted my spirits enormously, to know I was

appreciated, at least by the fans,' says Gardner. 'And I still had a dream to win the world championship, even if it seemed a hell of a way off at that stage. While I seriously considered retirement, every time it got down to the fact that there was this deep ambition gnawing at me. I had to keep going no matter what the odds. It was as simple as that.'

CHAPTER 8

Self-sponsorship

Wayne Gardner watches a lot of television. He doesn't enjoy reading, so watching the box provides much of his relaxation. He'll watch just about anything, from games shows to movies. In the hours immediately before a race, Gardner likes to sit alone in his motorhome watching television or a video movie as he prepares himself mentally for the task ahead. In those times he doesn't remember much of what he has seen, but finds the distraction of the screen comforting. Donna's mother videotapes Australian serials and sends them over to Europe, and Wayne even enjoys watching the commercials because they remind him of Australia. At home in Monaco he sits through endless hours of reruns of second-rate 1960s American shows because there is nothing else to watch on the English-language satellite television station. You could describe him as a television addict. He loves it.

However, Gardner didn't enjoy what he was watching on the evening of 24 March 1984. He and Donna were sitting at home at the comfortable bungalow they had bought two years previously in the Lincolnshire village of Wragby. Gardner had had a big win in the British TT Formula One championship that day at Thruxton to follow his first round win at Cadwell Park, but wasn't particularly satisfied. His brief taste of GP racing the previous year had only fuelled his appetite for more. The challenge had gone out of British racing to a great extent. He was only back doing the same old races on the same old circuits against the same old faces because a sponsor who had been lined up by Honda Britain to support a Grand Prix campaign had backed out at the last minute. That same day the world 500-cc championship first round was run at Kyalami in South Africa, and the highlights came on television that night. Gardner didn't like what he saw.

Rising Yamaha star Eddie Lawson won the race from French Honda ace Raymond Roche, with Barry Sheene third on a Suzuki. Fair enough, all were good riders, but the next seven places in the top ten were filled by riders Gardner knew he could beat—men like Sergio Pellandini, Massimo Broccoli, Christian le Liard and Chris Guy—riders who had done precious little then and have done little since. Gardner was completely frustrated, dreaming of going GP racing and confident he could run with the leading riders, but trapped in Britain.

'I pleaded with Barry Symmonds to allow me to do some GPs, and I know he was just as keen to do them as I was. Barry always wanted to go GP racing. He was always onto Gerald Davison [the Honda UK boss] to let us go GP racing but Davison would say "No, no, it's got nothing to do with us [in Britain]. Honda [Japan] has got its own factory GP team." Finally he must have relented because Barry told me we could get the bike and the spares, and Dunlop would supply the tyres, but I'd have to pay for the team to go to each race meeting,' Gardner recalls. And the GPs selected couldn't clash with racing commitments in Britain. 'I talked it over with Harris, and we decided if I didn't try I'd never know—just like when I left Australia. So basically we took the gamble. It cost me 15,000 pounds to do five GPs, or maybe it was closer to 16,000. Harris would know exactly—probably down to the last penny,' he says with a chuckle.

'Fortunately I did well. I finished fourth in the first GP at Misano in Italy, and third in Sweden. I ended up getting back 12,000 pounds in prize money so I just about broke even. To me, it was well worth it.'

Gardner laughs when he remembers that trip to Italy for the race at Misano on 15 April 1984. 'Honda had booked us into the same hotel as the factory team, but when I discovered that it would set me back 700 pounds we soon moved out into cheaper accommodation. Even so, that first race cost me 2800 pounds.'

When official practice started, Gardner shocked everyone by recording second fastest time behind Honda's number one, Freddie Spencer—an effort particularly remarkable because he was on a production RS500 Honda, considerably down on horsepower compared to Spencer's V4 and all the other works

Gardner's first Grand Prix victory—on the rostrum with Eddie Lawson (left) *and Mike Baldwin* (right) *at Jarama in Spain, 1986* (Don Morley)

Spraying the Moet after winning the 1986 Dutch Grand Prix with Randy Mamola (left) *and Mike Baldwin* (Rothmans Press Service)

Delighted with victory in a very wet British Grand Prix at Silverstone in 1986 (Rothmans Press Service)

Hard at work on the world championship-winning Rothmans Honda in the Italian Grand Prix at Monza, 1987 (Rothmans Press Service)

bikes in the field. Gardner showed it was no flash in the pan by going even faster on the second day of practice, to claim third spot on the grid behind Spencer and Lawson, and ahead of the likes of established GP stars Roche, Haslam, Sheene and Virginio Ferrari. Spencer won the race from Lawson and Roche, with Gardner home in an impressive fourth place. Franco Uncini, back racing after his near-fatal crash the previous year, was fifth, twelve seconds behind Gardner. This time there was no-one telling the young Australian he wasn't good enough to be there.

Gardner might have proved something to himself and the GP world, but it made no difference. He had to return to Britain and fulfil his commitments there and didn't get another GP start until the Dutch race at Assen on 30 June. Meanwhile, Gardner took out his frustrations on his British championship rivals—demoralising all comers with a string of victories. He won the Shell Oils British 500-cc championship with four wins from five races, the TT F1 title with eight victories from nine starts, and the Masters championship.

Symmonds is convinced that paying his own way to the GPs was 'character-building' for Gardner. In an interview in the British Road Racer magazine in 1988, Symmonds said he believed putting the new boy through a year of financing a GP effort enabled them to achieve a lot more subsequently than they otherwise would have done. Symmonds believes if Honda Britain had gone straight into GP racing in '84 with Gardner as a fully supported rider, it would have erected barriers between him and the other competitors. Instead, Wayne was able to moan with the best of them about the price of diesel and the appetites of his mechanics. He could also talk to the other riders without being perceived as a threat. 'I remember him sitting down with Eddie Lawson at Hockenheim for a long, long time, and Wayne doesn't miss a trick. If something's mentioned it's logged away, then he'll check it out and use it for information,' Symmonds said in the interview.

Gardner concedes Symmonds's point to some extent, but it still rankles with him that he had to wait so long to break into GP racing when others with lesser talent had rides. 'But I guess it made me hungrier for success when I finally got a full-time ride,' he says. 'I'm still as hungry for success as I was five years ago. When I go out on the track, coming second is losing. I want to win every time. You have to go into each race with that attitude, or it is time to give it away. If you don't go out there to try your hardest to win, there is a much higher risk of losing concentration and maybe crashing and hurting yourself.'

And he knows exactly what Symmonds means about pumping the established stars for information. It's why even now he gives nothing away about his riding, to anybody. He reasons that he did it the hard way, on his own, and he is not going to give anyone else an easy ride to the top.

Back at Assen in 1984, a year after the Uncini crash, Gardner made light of the pressure he was feeling. The section of track where the accident had occurred had been cut from the circuit, and was now part of an access road to the pits. It sent a shudder down Gardner's spine each day as he drove to the track, and still does even now. The horror of that crash is etched deeply in his mind. The 1984 Dutch GP holds much happier memories. Gardner finished fifth in the race, then followed that up with seventh place the next weekend in the Belgian Grand Prix at the notorious Spa-Francorchamps Circuit—an ultra-fast ribbon of bitumen cut out of a pine-clad hillside in the magnificent Ardennes mountains. It's every bit as daunting as it looks, and Gardner was happy to finish seventh, and in one piece. At the British GP at Silverstone, Gardner finished sixth and moved into seventh place in the world championship from just four starts.

Inspired by that effort, Honda helped Gardner get to the Swedish GP and supplied him with a factory NS500 engine to replace the production powerplant he had been using. It was Gardner's first taste of factory horsepower and he loved it, bringing the Honda home in third place behind Lawson's Yamaha and Roche's Honda. Final points for the season saw Gardner seventh in the world championship from his five races of the twelve, just one point behind Sheene. He came home to Australia to contest the Swann Series for the first time since 1981, convinced he had done enough to clinch a full-time GP ride for 1985. As if to underline his confidence, he wrapped up the Swann Series with little trouble.

Gardner's confidence seemed to be well placed. An

English businessman who ran a computer and communications company was prepared to pour hundreds of thousands of pounds into sponsoring a Honda Britain/Wayne Gardner assault on the world championship. However, the money, and the businessman, soon melted away like a mirage. Even now, Gardner doesn't like talking about how he was taken in by the businessman's promises. 'He was a bullshit artist,' is all he would say on the matter. Donna was more forthcoming, however. 'When we went to his house it was a little tenement. He said he was waiting for the new one to be built, and we thought "Oh yeah, here we go." When he stopped turning up in his Rolls Royce and started driving around in a little car, and saying the Roller was in the shop, we knew things were going wrong.' Gardner had been the victim of a confidence trickster.

Gardner was disillusioned and disappointed. He couldn't countenance another season racing in Britain, and was considering switching to Superbike racing in the United States or retiring altogether—both drastic steps considering how close he was to achieving his dream of full-time world championship riding. All was not lost, however. Uncini had decided to retire, and his Italian Suzuki boss Roberta Gallina flew Gardner and Barnett from London to Genoa in north-western Italy for a secret meeting to discuss a contract for 1985. The acrimony over the Uncini crash apparently forgotten, Gallina offered Gardner full backing, including an apartment in Italy, a car and a motorhome. There was one drawback. Suzuki had ceased its Grand Prix development programme and Gallina's bikes were unlikely to be competitive. Gardner decided getting onto a slow bike for his first full year of GP racing was a backward step, and declined the offer.

By this time, Honda was alarmed at the prospect of losing one of its rising stars, and took steps to make sure he stayed with the company. Rothmans had just started a sponsorship deal with the official factory team of Freddie Spencer, Randy Mamola and Japanese ace Takazumi Katayama. The sponsorship umbrella would be widened to allow a Rothmans Honda Britain team of Gardner and Ron Haslam to contest the 1985 season on factory NS500s. One man who is convinced Gardner made the right move to decline the Suzuki offer is Spaniard Sito Pons, the number-one 250-cc rider in the world at the time of writing. Pons took the ride on the Gallina Suzuki in 1985 after Gardner declined, and had a miserable year. His best result was seventh in the French GP, and he finished just four of the twelve races for eleven championship points and twelfth place overall. Speaking at Phillip Island before the 1989 Australian Grand Prix, Pons said, 'It was a very difficult year. The bike was very slow and I didn't get any good results. I think it was good luck for Wayne that he stuck with Honda.' Good luck, and good riding.

CHAPTER 9

Hitting the Big Time

Factory riders are the elite of motorcycle sport. The privateers battle to get to each race on an outdated machine, second-rate tyres and the bare minimum of a team—maybe two mechanics, and a wife or girlfriend to record the times. More often than not, the privateers' sponsorship is so low that, by the time all their expenses have been accounted for, it actually costs them money to compete. They have absolutely no chance of winning a GP, but try their hardest each race with just one object in mind: catching the eye of a team boss in the hope that they will be invited to ride for a factory the next year. If they do, they join the big league with six- or seven-figure contracts; a team of three or four mechanics to work on the bikes; frame, suspension and engine experts; the best tyres; publicity staff; and enough money to buy a luxury motorhome and employ someone to drive it from track to track. You would expect life to be a breeze for a factory rider, but actually getting on the bike is just one part of the job; there are also numerous media and sponsors' duties to perform. And there is no room for failure.

With factory support for a full world championship season in 1985, Gardner had hit the big time at last. However, it didn't take long for the reality to sink in that life was considerably different from his days spent racing in Britain. In fact, his life wasn't his own any more. Out on the racetrack, results were demanded. Gardner could handle that—he had always set high standards for himself and it all fitted in with his ambition to be the best rider in the world. Off the track, however, it was a different matter. Barry Symmonds's first instruction was that Donna had to stay at home in Australia. The Honda Britain team boss said having a girlfriend along was too much of a distraction. It was to be a make-or-break year and Gardner had to concentrate solely on his racing. Donna would have to go.

Donna accepted the decision reluctantly, but admits at the time she had begun to feel like 'excess baggage'. 'In our first year in England I used to do all the little things—clean his leathers, helmet and boots, things like that, just like his Mum had done in Australia,' she says. 'If he fell off, I'd bathe his grazes and patch him up, and generally help out during practice sessions with time-keeping and so on. But things changed. There was someone for every job. If he fell off in practice he'd be whisked off to a specialist before I'd even realised something had happened. I wasn't doing much more than putting out clean underpants for him.'

At the beginning of 1985, Donna stayed home in Australia and completed a beautician's course. It lasted until mid-season, when Gardner had had enough of the forced separation and asked Donna to come back to Europe. When she arrived, he took three days off for a romantic weekend in Paris. He says the break made him realise how much he needed Donna 'to keep me human', and how much he wanted her with him. Donna has been by his side at almost every race since then. 'Donna keeps me in touch with reality. If she thinks I'm getting too big for my boots she tells me. Sometimes, with all the media hype and the fans at the racetrack, it is easy to get carried away by it all but Donna makes sure this doesn't happen,' Gardner says.

He had his first ride in the blue-and-white Rothmans colours at Suzuka on 10 March 1985 at the annual Japanese season pipe-opener, the Two Plus Four. The Honda Racing Corporation bosses made it quite clear that victory was the expected result. The reality of having factory bikes hit home. Riding for Honda Britain on production machinery that was available to any privateer with the money to buy it meant he had been answerable only to his team boss. When he was entered on machinery provided by the factory racing division it was a whole new ball game. Success was all that mattered. Determined to do well at the Two Plus Four, Gardner didn't let anyone down, least of all himself. He won the 500-cc race on an NS500 GP bike and took out the Formula One event on an RVF750 four-stroke, setting new lap records in both. The two victories also started a sequence of nine consecutive wins in Japan, earning him a huge fan following and the nickname there of Mr Hundred Per Cent.

The 1985 world 500-cc championship started at Kyalami in South Africa on 24 March. Gardner earned a United Nations blacklisting for competing in the republic, but wasn't in the least worried about that. As far as he was concerned his job was to race motorcycles, and he'd go anywhere he was required. Political issues do not weigh heavily on his mind. Apart from the blacklisting, Gardner also earned himself ten championship points with third place behind the American world champions of the two previous years, Honda's Freddie Spencer and Yamaha's Eddie Lawson. That was much more important.

The South African Grand Prix also established a pattern that was to continue all through the season. Lawson and Spencer, along with French Yamaha riders Christian Sarron and Raymond Roche, had V4 engines in their bikes while most of the other competitive riders such as Gardner, Haslam, Mamola and Belgian Didier de Radigues were on three-cyclinder Hondas. The triples were fast and agile, but no match for the V4s in outright horsepower. At most races, Spencer and Lawson could simply power away from the field, leaving the 'second division' to scrap for the minor placings. It's a far cry from the current situation. In the 1989 world championship, Honda went in with six riders on factory V4s, Yamaha with six, Suzuki two and Cagiva one. Grand Prix motorcycle racing has expanded considerably in a few short years.

'1985 was a big race between the three cylinder guys— Randy, Ronnie and myself. I knew I had no chance of winning the world championship, but I always like to set myself a target that is one level above a realistic goal, something achievable but that I still have to push myself to get. I set myself the goal of beating all the other three cylinders and trying to finish in the first three as often as possible, which would mean having to beat some of the V4s. I set myself the goal of coming third or fourth in the championship and beating all the other three cylinders, and I did that,' Gardner says. 'We were battling it out week after week, knowing a win was very unlikely, unless something happened to the top guys. But there was a lot of pride in being the first three-cylinder home, and a lot at stake as well. We all figured the top guys in our group would get

V4 rides in 1986. And of course there was a lot of satisfaction in beating riders on the same machinery as you, even if you knew you couldn't actually win the GP. You could win your own private race within the race.'

After Kyalami, Gardner was made an 'honorary Pom' and drafted into the British team for the transatlantic Match Races against the United States at Easter. The factories wouldn't let Spencer and Lawson ride, so once again it was a private war between Haslam and Gardner for Britain and Mamola for the United States. The Australian didn't have anywhere near the experience of Haslam or Mamola, but won the three races run in the dry including a fierce, fairing-bashing duel at Donington with Mamola. His victories helped the British team win the series 336-254, but more importantly they established a psychological advantage over the other two riders that he was to hold for the rest of the season.

On 5 May the riders returned to the real thing, round two of the world championship at Jarama in Spain. Honda's founder, Soichiro Honda, flew in by helicopter to watch his riders, and the pressure to perform was intense. Gardner qualified third on the grid, just one tenth of a second behind pole-sitter Eddie Lawson, with the next group of riders two seconds behind them. However, the race was an entirely different story, with Gardner forced off the track by de Radigues on lap three. 'The bike fell over but I managed to keep the engine running while it was on its side. When I got it upright again I grabbed a big handful of throttle and the back wheel promptly dug a big hole. I finally got out in twenty-eighth spot, so I decided to just put my head down and go for it. I went mad.' Gardner picked up place after place and eventually finished fourth in an heroic effort, coming home behind the V4s of Spencer, Lawson and Sarron. On his lap times, he probably would have finished second had he not run off the track. 'Eddie Lawson came up to me afterwards and told me I had what it takes. That's all he said, but it meant more to me than the world championship points. I mean, he was the defending world champion and he was telling me I was up there, on that level. I was over the moon.'

That was the last time Gardner received any direct encouragement from another rider. Certainly Spencer, then the senior Honda rider, offered nothing in the way of support in 1985. If anything, he studiously ignored the Australian. And, as Gardner became increasingly competitive and consistent, the other leading riders, who all happened to be American, turned their backs on him. 'They were starting to be afraid of me by then. They could see if I got a fast bike I would be a threat to their own title hopes. They were starting . . . well, not to be nasty to me, but not to be very nice either.'

At this point, Donna chimes in: 'We never really fitted in. They never invited us to dinner, or to join them on the golf course or anything like that. Never. When Wayne started to be a big threat, that was it. They really didn't want to know him. I always have the feeling the Americans don't want to know those they can't dominate.' Gardner agrees: 'The Americans like the other guys because they don't have a mind of their own. They go around like a bunch of sheep, and hang around the American riders, going motocrossing with them in the off-season, that kind of thing. The Americans know they can squash them into the ground. And guys like that never win. But I won't stand for that, because I've got a mind of my own. I want to be totally different, and they don't like that.'

Of course it is not all one-sided. Gardner studiously keeps himself aloof from most of the other riders because he feels it is a sign of weakness to be too friendly to his rivals. He also is deeply suspicious that, by getting close to him, other riders are simply trying to probe him for personal weaknesses and glean information about his machine. 'I believe if you're with them all the time, you're giving stuff away. Without knowing it, you're giving things away that you shouldn't—maybe they can see how you think, how you might get beaten, what makes you feel sad, any of those things. And I don't want to give anything like that away. It's a psych game, and you have to play it hard. I've worked too hard for what I've got, just to give it away. The real top guys don't mix so much, because they're competitive. I mean, the press made a lot of me and Eddie not having much to do with each other, but you have to remember we were out there racing against each other most weeks. We both wanted to win very badly, so it was pretty hard to be best friends off the track, during the season anyway. Respect sure, friendship not so much.'

Even when fellow Australian Kevin Magee joined the GP circus in 1988, Gardner didn't embrace him with open arms. He was friendly, but his professionalism forced him to hold back. When Magee signed with the Lucky Strike Yamaha, he became a rival just like anyone else. Nevertheless, some sections of the Australian motorcycle press seemed to think it was wrong of Gardner not to rush over to the Yamaha team at every opportunity and help Magee out during his first season, showing him the tracks and generally offering advice. This was a ridiculous proposition, and when the opposite happened there were all sorts of rumours of rifts between the two. One article in particular, in an Australian magazine, alleged Gardner was too big-headed to talk to the new Australian rider. It hurt Gardner deeply. 'What was I expected to do—take Kevin on a guided tour of every track and show him the fast lines? I'm sure Honda wouldn't have been impressed with me if I'd done that. People forget that I was on a Honda and Kevin was on a Yamaha. There's a lot at stake here, and the factories don't give anything away. As it happens, I like Kevin a lot but I still want to beat him every time, just as I am sure he wants to beat me.'

Of his fellow Grand Prix riders, Gardner best enjoys the company of jovial Scotsman Niall MacKenzie, while he has high regard for Ron Haslam and Christian Sarron. Didier de Radigues also lives in Monaco, where Gardner has lived since 1987, and the pair have formed a close friendship, water-skiing and boating together. Even so, Gardner admits he 'doesn't give anything away about racing'.

Gardner certainly gave the other riders reason to feel threatened in 1985. He served notice he was the hottest new property on the GP scene and destined for greater things. His first full season of GP racing saw him consistently on the rostrum, with third placings at Mugello in the Italian Grand Prix, Rijeka in Yugoslavia and Assen in Holland. Marlboro Yamaha team boss Giacomo Agostini, the legendary Italian who had won 122 GPs in the 3540-cc and 500-cc classes, as well as eight world 500-cc titles, wanted Gardner in his team for 1986 as a team-mate or replacement for Eddie Lawson. Honda reacted swiftly by flying Gardner to Japan to ride a 500-cc V4 at a mid-season meeting at Suzuka. Gardner won the 500-cc race, as well as the Suzuka

200-kilometre endurance race on an RVF750 Honda. The factory promised him a V4 for the British GP on 4 August. He returned to Europe for the French GP at Le Mans on 21 July, and showed he could still manage pretty well on his V3.

The French GP holds bitter-sweet memories. Gardner should have won, but a disintegrating rear tyre robbed him of victory. However, he demonstrated to himself and the rest of the GP world his considerable and growing talent. He may not have finished the race, but his performance convinced him that he could match the top riders.

The bikes use the short circuit at the legendary Le Mans circuit north-west of Paris. The infamous 5-kilometre-long Mulsanne Straight is by-passed because it would be absolutely lethal for these 300-kilometre-per-hour racing motorcycles. The result is a fairly tight circuit, with virtually no straight sections apart from a short drag past the pits. Its numerous bends and changes of direction make it a real rider's circuit, where riding ability can count for more than outright horsepower. In the 1985 race it meant the V3s could be just about as competitive as the V4s—in the right hands. Gardner qualified fourth on the grid behind Spencer, Lawson and Sarron, but went to the lead on lap four. Spencer caught him and hit the front on lap eight, with the Australian hot on his heels and back in the lead a few laps later. This time the American couldn't get back, and Gardner started to pull away. Gardner could almost taste the champagne of his first GP victory, but it went decidedly flat on lap fourteen. His rear tyre disintegrated and he was forced out, leaving Spencer to win by sixteen seconds.

Gardner didn't have time to lament his ill fortune. Straight after the race he was whisked away and onto a flight to Tokyo for the Suzuka Eight-hour race the next weekend. The Eight-hour is unquestionably Japan's biggest motor sport event, and carries enormous prestige in the important domestic Japanese motorcycle market. There were 250,000 spectators at Suzuka in 1985 to witness the clash between Honda's rising star, Gardner, and the legendary American ace, Kenny Roberts—the three-times world 500-cc champion who had come out of retirement to win the race for Yamaha. The Japanese fans idolise the top riders, flocking to the racetracks dressed as replicas of their heroes in identical leather suits and helmets. The Japanese liken the racetrack duels to the image of the samurai, but the modern-day warriors' weapons are powerful motorcycles rather than swords.

It can be incredibly hot and humid in Japan in July, and race day at Suzuka was a sweltering thirty-six degrees. When the race started, Gardner took the attack right to Roberts but his Honda partner Masaki Tokuno wasn't on the pace, and the lead see-sawed between the two teams, with Gardner riding his heart out during his stints to make up for his partner's poor times. With one hour to go Roberts held a narrow advantage with his co-rider, Japanese Yamaha number one Tadahiko Taira, out on the bike. Gardner elected to do the last two hours by himself, brushing aside the waiting Tokuno at the final fuel stop to continue his relentless pursuit of the Yamaha. Taira reacted to frantic signals from his pit crew and upped his pace, but the pressure was too much and his engine gave up with a bent valve thirty minutes before the finish. Gardner won and the crowd went wild, spilling across the track in a human tide as he crossed the finish line. Gardner, already semi-delirious and completely exhausted from the gruelling race in the intense heat, collapsed as the fans reached him. Roger Marshall and his mechanics had to rush to his rescue, carrying him shoulder-high through the crowd back to the pits, where he needed treatment in an oxygen tent. The victory was an enormous boost to Gardner's career, delighting the Honda hierarchy and cementing his relationship with the factory.

It was definitely a high point of the season, but things weren't so rosy on the Grand Prix front. At a very wet British GP at Silverstone the following weekend, aboard the promised V4, Gardner was forced out of the race after just five laps due to a badly fogged visor. A week later at Anderstorp in Sweden, he was back on the V3 and chasing Spencer hard when disaster struck again. He was holding second going into the final lap, eight seconds ahead of third-placed Lawson, when his Honda ran out of petrol and he coasted to a halt within sight of the chequered flag. However, at the final race of the year, the San Marino GP at Misano in Italy, Gardner finished second to wrap up fourth place in the championship behind Spencer, Lawson and Sarron—fulfilling his aim of heading the V3 riders.

Traditionally, the final GP of the year is also the official start of the saddle-swapping 'silly season', and Gardner was the hottest property on the market. Spencer was tied to Rothmans Honda, and Lawson to Marlboro Yamaha for 1986, so Gardner was the man all the team managers wanted to talk to. It was obvious there would no longer be any concern about whether he would have a ride; it was now a matter of which factory offer to choose. He and Harris Barnett had plenty to consider. Agostini renewed his approach for Marlboro Yamaha, Gallina was interested again, and the wealthy Italian Cagiva team also put in a bid. But when it came down to the crunch, there were just two players—the Rothmans Honda factory team and a new operation formed by Kenny Roberts, the Lucky Strike Yamaha team. Roberts was a long-time Gardner admirer, further impressed by his whole-hearted effort at Suzuka in the Eight-hour. Although his sponsorship by the American tobacco company Lucky Strike stipulated that he use American riders, Roberts was prepared to make an exception if he could get Gardner. And Roberts was prepared to pay $750,000 for his signature.

Gardner underlined his value to Honda with a win in the non-championship Japanese Grand Prix in October, then was given Spencer's V4 for a race against Lawson in Malaysia. He won again, much to Lawson's disgust. After the race, Lawson headed straight for the airport instead of the victory rostrum. Despite those wins, Honda was reluctant to match Roberts's offer, coming up with a reported $600,000 deal. Gardner accepted the lower fee to stay with Honda, reasoning that his four-year relationship with the biggest motorcycle manufacturer in the world could develop into an important long-term career. 'The money wasn't as good as Kenny's offer but money isn't everything. I had a good relationship with the Honda factory by that time and I wanted to build on that. I also had a clause in my contract guaranteeing me identical machinery and support to Freddie Spencer, so I thought Honda gave me my best chance of challenging for the world championship.' He celebrated signing as a fully-fledged Honda factory rider by bringing the V4 to Australia for the Swann Series, and winning it again.

CHAPTER 10
Mind Games

Shrinks, brain benders, mind minders—whatever you call them, sports psychologists draw mixed responses. Magic, or mumbo-jumbo, people swear by them, scorn them or fear them. But like them or not, they are here to stay. It is simply a reality, in these days of multi-million-dollar sports, vast worldwide audiences, enormous sponsorship opportunities and awesome pressure to succeed, that competitors and their backers will explore every avenue for a road to the top. One of those avenues is sports psychology, with competitors seeking help to tap unknown depths of inner strength and talent, or to correct a fault. Success in sport requires much more than natural talent. Certainly, you have to get the physical side right, but a tennis player who crashes when holding three match points or a soccer player who shoots wide from three metres knows only too well that when the mind isn't working right, the body may not work at all. Sporting history is littered with the corpses of individuals or teams who could not leap a final hurdle to achieve greatness. Thus a tennis star may use a sports psychologist to erase a phobia about a certain opponent, or a golfer may seek help to overcome a case of the putting 'yips'.

There's another side too. Sponsors may want to be sure their person is mentally suitable for the job before they sign him or her up—that their money is being well spent. That is precisely why Wayne Gardner caught a train from London to the genteel glades of Ascot late in 1985. Rothmans had just such a test in mind for him before they were prepared to sign him up for the Rothmans Honda factory team for 1986. Waiting for him at Ascot was Phil Fearon, a quiet, greying man in his mid-fifties with a considerable reputation for picking sportspeople who were capable of going all the way to the top, then helping them to get there. A psychologist and retired college headmaster, Fearon had started working with golfers before helping Konrad Bartelski become Britain's most successful skier ever. He had then turned his attention to motor sports, helping turn Ari Vatanen and Henri Toivonen into world champion rally drivers and devising personality tests to show major Formula One sponsors like Marlboro whether talented drivers had that extra mental strength to become the best. Niki Lauda, Rene Arnoux, Patrick Tambay and Stefano Modena are just four who have completed his tests for Marlboro. Rothmans had used Fearon for their rally team since 1980, and so asked him to assess Wayne Gardner.

The young Australian was terrified. 'When Rothmans told me they wanted me to see this guy to be evaluated, I panicked. I didn't know what to expect, I didn't want to go,' Gardner remembers. 'They sent me down to Ascot in the train and I was thinking all the way about the classic shrink situation—the long couch, taking me back to the womb and all that sort of thing. But of course it was nothing like that. We just sat and talked, very friendly, then he put me through a three-hour questionnaire about all sorts of general things to see how I would react in certain situations—whether I would push an old lady under a car, or help her across the road . . . that sort of thing,' he laughs.

Fearon remembers the first meeting just as vividly. 'Wayne's record showed he had tremendous potential, but it seemed obvious that he hadn't applied himself at school as much as he should have done. Perhaps that was the motorbike experience coming in. I wanted to test him on his intelligence, but he did lack a bit of confidence in formal work and questionnaires and I had to get through that and find out what was behind him. What the tests showed me was that he was a highly intelligent young man. I think if you look at the great champions in most sports, one of the qualities they've got is intelligence—and Wayne has a high intelligence. This was one of the qualities I was looking for, to be truthful. He also had natural aggression and a lot of competitiveness in him. A lot of very positive things came out: he is emotionally stable, he can face reality with sense and maturity, he's quite assertive in his approach on the track and he's very serious about his work, very conscientious. There were a whole lot of factors like that, and he certainly had an inner drive, motivation, to be the top. Wayne's results were very positive, and I said to Rothmans if you haven't signed this lad, sign him quickly, because he is a future world champion.'

Fearon admits there were some weaknesses, particularly what he calls a chip on Gardner's shoulder about the hard road he had been forced to take to reach the top, compared with some of the Americans and Europeans whose inferior talent was rewarded earlier with factory machinery and support. 'Wayne did have a chip on his shoulder about being Australian and having to prove himself all the time. We had to turn that into something positive,' Fearon recalls. 'He also wasn't very analytical about his own performance and I had to get through to him on that. I remember asking what he did during practice for a race, and Wayne replied "Practice makes perfect." I told him it didn't, that practice made permanent, and poor practice would result in bad habits becoming permanent. Only perfect practice makes perfect, so we started analysing practice sessions, working out lines and braking points and the like to try to make those practice sessions perfect.'

Gardner agrees that under Fearon's influence he began analysing aspects of his riding and race preparation that he had not consciously thought about before. 'Sometimes before a race I'd get so flustered and panicky about what to do, but Phil would break it down and point out that there was nothing to worry about—that I was as good as the other riders and they would be having the same problems and hassles as me. If I just kept to my routine and concentrated on my own performance, I'd do well in the race.'

Fearon also started Gardner keeping a diary on each race to be used a year later when he returned to the same track. 'Phil started me doing bookwork about my racing and I think I'm the only one who does it. I keep maps of the circuits, and go through the maps—then I write down all my thoughts about things such as gearboxes, suspension, carburation, braking. I do it at the end of each session with the team manager, basically breaking the bike down into sections and analysing it and how it could be changed or improved. Then we try it again the next session, and if it doesn't work, I note that down too. Phil's also

A world champion at last—tears and champagne with Donna and Randy Mamola on the rostrum after winning the 1987 Brazilian Grand Prix, and the world title (Rothmans Press Service)

Number one—and proud of it. Calder Park test session in Australia at the beginning of the 1988 season (Rothmans Press Service)

Cranked over during the Spanish Grand Prix, Jerez, 1988 (Franco Villani)

Heading for victory in front of a massive crowd at the Dutch Grand Prix, Assen, 1988 (Rothmans Press Service)

taught me a lot about visualisation. I can look at a circuit map and visualise the race the next day, what's going to happen in certain circumstances and how to approach that if it happens, even down to going for the finish line close to someone else, thinking about what I can do to beat him.'

Not surprisingly, Gardner's great rival over the past few years, Eddie Lawson, looms largest in his visualisations. 'It is amazing how visualisation can create something that actually happens, and then you're prepared for it. Obviously I visualise situations with the most competitive riders—sometimes two or three, but sometimes just Eddie. I think about his weaknesses, and what I can do to exploit them in a certain situation. Phil's slogan is "Plan to work, work to plan" and I try to follow that through. I like to walk a circuit before practice starts, standing at corners thinking about where to change gear and start braking and so on. If I've gone well at a certain track, Phil encourages me to follow the same routine the next year—down to what I ate or drank, what time I went to bed each night, that sort of thing. He wants me to try to re-create the environment that brought me success the previous year, although obviously that isn't always possible.'

Fearon preaches a doctrine which all but ignores the other riders. 'I work on the person I'm working on, and ignore the opposition. Obviously there comes a time when you have to consider the opposition but you've got no control over other peoples' performance. However, you do have control over your own, and giving you control over your own performance is giving you self-control, teaching you how to manipulate your talents. That's what I'd prefer to work on, rather than imponderables over which I've got no control, and over which the rider has no control. So we concentrate on what he's got to do.' Yet Fearon admits that he likes to play on the other riders' fears about Gardner. Obviously, as one of the great riders of the last five years, Gardner is a respected rival, but Fearon likes to take it further. 'At the British Grand Prix in 1988 Wayne had a very heavy fall in practice, when he was thrown right over the handlebars and landed heavily on the track. His team wanted him to stop but I told him to get back out on the track. He agreed, although he needed pain-killers to do it. But the message we wanted to get across to the other riders was that nothing would stop Wayne racing. He'd already raced that season with broken bones in his foot, and we wanted to show that he was too tough to beat, that he was the toughest man in the race.'

Fearon is also strict on self-concept. He says Gardner is at the top of his sport, and should never forget it. He should make it work in his favour, by intimidating his opponents. He was annoyed that Gardner hadn't booked into the best hotel on the Monterey Peninsula for the first United States Grand Prix at Laguna Seca, California, in 1988. Gardner made sure he was booked there the next year.

According to Fearon, Gardner's greatest attribute is that he will not be beaten. 'If it is in his power to produce a winning performance, he'll produce it. But he's also gained so much self-control, so much discipline in his riding. Obviously the intention is to win every race, but he knows that sometimes when he goes out another rider might be on a hot streak, or his own machinery might not be good enough. Then he just does the best he can under the circumstances. But if there is a chance he can win, he won't be beaten. However, perhaps what I like most about him is that he's not interested in winning just for the sake of it. Don't get me wrong: he's very, very interested in winning, but he wants to contribute to the sport. He feels he's had a lot out of the sport and he wants to give something back to the spectators and fans. That certainly gives me added respect for him, and it's one of the reasons I like working with him.'

The Gardner/Fearon partnership had its first test at Jarama in Spain early in May 1986 at the first round of that year's world championship. Gardner was having his first start as an official factory rider, albeit as junior team-mate to the defending world champion Freddie Spencer, and Fearon was on hand to help out. 'We worked out a strategy for practice and Wayne did his fastest lap ever around Jarama. He was really pleased, but then he abandoned our plans and tried to go faster his way. He was half a second slower. When he came in I told him he was an idiot, and asked why he had done it. He replied that he just wanted to see for himself if what I had told him really was the best way, and he had satisfied himself that it was,' Fearon recalls. 'I was pleased that he had done that. He was suspicious of me and my methods, and he had to check them.'

Nevertheless, Gardner had a major crash in practice, when the bike high-sided him over the handlebars, then chased him along the track before slamming him in the back of the head. It was a vicious blow to Gardner's confidence, and Fearon recalls talking him through the accident afterwards. 'He assured me he was alright but it was quite obvious he wasn't. (That's another characteristic he has: he's a real fighter. Perhaps that's the Australian in him—he'll get up from any accident and give his best.) I didn't expect him to do well. However, I devised a positive scheme for him to forget about his accident and he went out for the rest of practice with a set of instructions he had to stick to. He achieved a good time and ended up second on the grid behind Spencer, and so he went into the race with renewed confidence.'

Spencer made his customary lightning start and after a few laps had drawn away from a scrap between Lawson's Yamaha and Gardner's Honda. However, by lap ten Gardner was clear of Lawson and starting to eat into Spencer's lead. By lap fourteen he was on Spencer's rear wheel and poised to pass the American for the lead, when Spencer 'cried "enough" ' and pulled into the pits. He blamed tendonitis in his right wrist, but Gardner, Fearon, and quite a few others were convinced the Australian would have won the race whether Spencer was fit or not. 'Freddie retired from the race because of his tendonitis, but I don't think it made any difference, because Wayne was really going, and flowing, and I feel he was unbeatable on that day. That result certainly established our respect for each other,' says Fearon. Gardner's victory was the first 500-cc Grand Prix won by an Australian in nine years.

Gardner has always had reservations about allowing his association with a sports psychologist to be widely known. In fact, it was a closely guarded secret throughout the first year, and the Grand Prix grapevine, usually so quick with rumours of both fact and fiction, remained silent. The distinguished-looking gentleman who occasionally turned up at a racetrack dressed in Rothmans Honda gear was generally assumed to be a Rothmans executive, or a friend of Harris Barnett. Both Gardner and Fearon took care to keep their consultations private, usually in a hotel room away from the track, and Gardner made sure he never mentioned them to the press. It wasn't until three years later that the association became general knowledge. 'I guess I was embarrassed about what people would think of me using a "shrink",' Gardner acknowledges. 'I didn't even really want my parents to know about it at first. But then I thought "What the heck, if Martina Navratilova can use one without anyone batting an eyelid then why should motorcycle racing be any different from tennis?" I guess because I was really the first one to get into this sort of thing, I was worried about the reaction from the other riders and the fans. I certainly didn't shout it from the rooftops, but by 1988 people were starting to get the general idea of what Phil was all about. I remember Eddie Lawson having a shot at me, saying if he had to use a shrink it wouldn't be worth racing. But now the American riders use Dean Miller, who supposedly works on the physical side of things, but I notice him pumping them up mentally as well.'

Fearon understands the embarrassment, but says the sportsmen who really have the desire to reach the top are more willing to listen to sports psychologists. 'They avail themselves of every opportunity to get to the top, and they're more willing to learn, more open to ideas. Although they may be suspicious, if they think you've got something to offer they'll take it . . . and you just have to win their confidence. They are the ones with the talent, and they know they've got the talent, so I make it clear from the outset that my job is in the background, that I'm no threat to them. But they often don't want their association with me made known—I suppose it is some sort of embarrassment, but they should not feel embarrassed. I'm just an added aid, nothing more.'

Gardner doesn't use Fearon all the time. In 1986 Fearon attended several races, but generally kept in the background. Gardner would phone him, or visit him at Ascot, but preferred to go to the racetrack alone and simply follow the routines they had formulated. In 1987, when Gardner won the world championship, Fearon didn't attend any races. 'I knew right from the start of 1987, when we were testing the new bike at Surfers Paradise, that I had a good machine. I knew that if I "planned to work, worked to plan", things would go well that year so

I didn't use Phil, although I did follow the routines we had built up together.' Fearon returned in 1988, when Gardner knew there would be added pressure on him as defending champion. He was entering uncharted waters and he wanted Fearon to act as a navigator. As it happened, machinery problems destroyed his season that year, and he had to be content with second place in the championship behind his old rival, Lawson.

That rivalry really began in 1986. All predictions for that year were based around a Spencer-Lawson, Honda-Yamaha dogfight between the two American superstars. However, the tendonitis Spencer experienced in the Spanish Grand Prix recurred throughout the season and he didn't finish a race. In fact, he rarely even started one. His supposed apprentice, Gardner, was forced to carry the fortunes of the mighty Honda factory alone. He had won the first race in Spain, followed by four Yamahas—Lawson, Mike Baldwin, Randy Mamola and Christian Sarron. He was like a fox being pursued by the hounds, and they were after his blood. Gardner began to feel isolated. Suddenly, from being very much the number-two rider in a learning year, he was thrust into the number-one role and became Honda's sole hope for winning the world championship. 'I didn't like it at all,' says Gardner. The Honda guys kept telling me not to let the situation worry me. They said there was no pressure to succeed, and just to ride my own race, but that made it worse. Everybody knew the pressure was there. I mean, at Honda Racing Corporation in Japan there are 200 workers whose only purpose is to produce a bike that wins the world championship . . . and all their efforts were riding with me. It was like being at the top of a giant pyramid.'

After the great victory in Spain, disaster struck at the next round of the '86 championship at Monza in Italy, when Gardner was struck on the start line by another bike, smashing his leg into the gear lever and leaving his knee swollen and very sore. The gear lever was also damaged, so Gardner had to return to the pits for repairs. He returned to the race a lap down to finish sixteenth, and out of the points. Lawson won the race to take over the championship lead, and from that moment Gardner was playing 'catch-up'. Lawson made it doubly difficult by stringing together four straight wins. By the time the GP circus reached Holland for the Dutch GP, Lawson had a mid-season lead of twenty-three points over Gardner, and the Australian was feeling the pressure. He arrived at Assen tense, nervous and not at all happy with the way he was riding.

This time he didn't call for Phil Fearon, but took a decidedly more traditional remedy. The boy from Wollongong took over from the cool, calculating professional racer, and he got drunk. Roger Marshall was at Assen with Honda Britain, and when he saw his Australian friend he knew he was struggling. 'As soon as I saw Wayne I knew something was up. There was no way he was enjoying his racing. He was too uptight, so I decided to do something about it,' says Marshall, who now runs a pub in Lincolnshire. 'I took him to a bar and made sure he got drunk.' The treatment worked. 'I felt bloody awful the next morning,' Gardner remembers. 'But once my head had cleared I felt like a huge weight had been lifted off my shoulders. We'd had a lot of beer and a lot of laughs and it made me realise there was more to racing than piling up championship points. I realised that if I was enjoying what I was doing I'd probably ride better, so I tried to relax more before each race.'

Gardner dominated the Dutch Grand Prix, taking the lead on lap two then running away with the race to win from Yamaha riders Randy Mamola and Mike Baldwin. The relief was evident as he flung his clenched fists in the air after he crossed the finish line. Lawson, uncharacteristically, had crashed on the first lap, so Gardner had cut his championship lead back to eight points. The title chase seemed wide open again, but it didn't work out that way. Lawson scored a second to Gardner's fourth in Belgium, then won the French GP at Paul Ricard while Gardner was pushed back to fifth by a wall of faster Yamahas.

Honda may have been concerned that Gardner wasn't winning, but Fearon wasn't. 'I don't necessarily look for wins. I look for good performance. If you haven't won but you can analyse your performance and see where you have improved, then that is something positive,' Fearon says. 'Wayne had a lot of learning of tracks to do in 1986 and I had him analysing them and getting to know them better, so that he could make a successful attempt at the world championship the following year. And that's what he did. He actually had an awful lot of learning to do, and that took his mind off the pressure a bit. I made sure he had a lot to do, and he did it extremely well. He was down at odd times, but I'd time my visits to see him when he was down and it seemed to work out well.'

Gardner kept the Honda hierarchy happy with a superb victory in the 1986 Suzuka Eight-hour race, which was run a week after the French GP. A crowd of 300,000 turned out to watch Gardner take on Kenny Roberts, but it was no contest. Back on his beloved RVF750 Honda, Gardner was thirty seconds ahead when he handed over to co-rider Dominique Sarron at the one-and-a-half-hour mark. Roberts's machine expired at the five-hour mark but by then Gardner and Sarron were so far ahead that victory was a formality. The win completed nine straight Gardner victories at Suzuka Circuit. His Japanese nickname of Mr Hundred Per Cent was well justified.

A week later Gardner was back on the other side of the world, lining up on pole position for a very wet British Grand Prix at Silverstone. Gardner was determined to lead on the first lap and force the others to ride into his spray, and the ploy worked. However, fellow Australian Paul Lewis had crashed his Suzuki at the first corner, and the marshals halted the race while the debris was cleared from the track. Gardner had to do it all over again—and he did, leading all the way for a memorable victory over Didier de Radigues and Lawson. The British Grand Prix was a race Gardner had dreamed of winning since arriving in England in 1981, and he was thrilled with the result. 'That win repaid a debt to Honda Britain and my old team manager, Barry Symmonds, in particular. They did so much for me in the four years I was with the team and it was great to repay them by winning at Silverstone. It was a nice way to say "thank you" to the British fans, too, because they had been very good to me over a long period and I considered myself half a Pom because of it.'

However, Lawson regained his composure to win the last two races of the year—the Swedish and San Marino GPs—and wrap up his second world championship. In both races Gardner, fittingly, finished second. The pair had dominated the season with Lawson winning seven of the eleven races, Gardner three and Mamola one. The championship table saw Lawson first on 139 points, followed by Gardner on 117 and Mamola on 105. Yamahas filled the first, third, fourth, fifth and sixth places, clearly demonstrating their superiority. Gardner had carried the Honda flag with distinction; but if he felt that entitled him to special consideration when contract negotiations started for the 1987 season, he was sadly mistaken. In fact, Honda's offer was hardly an improvement on the 1986 figure. Bitterly disappointed at what he saw as a slap in the face, Gardner was more than receptive to Kenny Roberts's renewed efforts to sign him for Lucky Strike Yamaha. Roberts was offering big money—around the million-dollar mark.

Gardner decided to change his strategy for dealing with the Japanese. In the past, Honda had insisted he discuss his contract with them face to face. Now he said no. Harris Barnett would carry out all negotiations on his behalf. He didn't want to see the Honda bosses until he was ready to sign, and he certainly wasn't ready to do that—not by a long way. In fact, Gardner returned to London and seemed set to sign with Roberts. Honda didn't take the threat seriously until it was almost too late, but when the racing executives realised their ace was about to change camps, they phoned a new offer through to Barnett in London. Two calls later Barnett heard what he wanted to hear, and he and Gardner were on the next plane to Tokyo to ink the contract. Eventually, Honda paid Gardner considerably more than Roberts had offered.

'I was sorry to turn down Kenny's offer for the second year and it was one of the toughest decisions I have ever had to make,' Gardner recalls. 'I wasn't happy with Honda because I didn't think they had placed any value on my second place in the world championship. In fact, their first offer was an insult and I told them that. I was very hurt that they didn't put a greater value on my efforts. But in the end the money from Honda was what I wanted, so it came down to machinery. I knew I could have a lot of input into the changes being made to the Honda bike for 1987 because I was really the only one racing the thing, and I knew Honda wanted to put in a really big effort to win back the championship. In the end, that's what swayed me, although it would also have been hard to break my association with Honda after five years. I was certainly tempted, though . . .'

CHAPTER 11

On Top of the World

The 1987 season was billed as the toughest ever in the history of Grand Prix motorcycle racing. There were fifteen races, four more than in 1986, spread across the world from Japan to Europe and to South America. But that didn't concern Wayne Gardner in the slightest. His whole career had been building towards this season, and he knew he could win the title. He was convinced his racing apprenticeship was over and he was ready to assume the role of the master— so convinced, in fact, that he didn't need Phil Fearon along to assist. Gardner had been racing for ten years, working hard and building up a vast knowledge of racecraft. In that time he had developed a deep hunger for the world title, and he was desperate to satisfy it. He was now Honda's number-one rider, so he had the machinery and technical backup to do the job. If he couldn't win in 1987, perhaps he never would.

Gardner left nothing to chance. He made sure the engineers at Honda Racing Corporation knew exactly what he wanted in the 1987 NSR500. As senior Honda rider, he had provided the major input into improvements to the 1986 bike, and team manager and fellow Australian Jerry Burgess spent most of January 1987 at HRC's headquarters near Tokyo supervising the changes. Gardner wanted smoother power delivery over a wider rev range to overcome the chronic wheelspin that had so hampered the 1986 NSR, constantly forcing the rear wheel to break traction and spin under hard acceleration out of corners. He also wanted a new, stronger frame and different steering geometry to improve handling and to overcome understeering problems on the exit from corners. What he wanted, he got. The 1987 NSR500 was one very mean motorcycle, and Gardner realised it as soon as he got on the bike.

'We were testing in Australia at Surfers Paradise, and

it took only a few laps for me to realise that the new bike was a hell of an improvement on the previous model,' he recalls. 'I thought we'd be in with a great chance of toppling Eddie for the world championship, because we had a bike that would match the Yamahas. It was quite a relief, because I had put so much into the bike and if it hadn't worked, my neck was on the line.' It was just as well Gardner was happy with the new bike from the start, because the team got precious little time to prepare themselves or the bike for the coming season.

They booked Surfers Paradise Circuit for a week early in February, and earnestly set about the considerable task of setting up a new machine and testing more than 300 tyre compounds for Michelin. But after two and a half days, Gardner's mind began to wander as he clocked up lap after lap in searing mid-summer heat on the track at Australia's most famous beach resort. He crashed, wrecking the bike and chipping a bone in his left ankle. The injury wiped out his pre-season test programme, and ruled him out of a race he planned to enter at Suzuka early in March.

'That was a blow, but it's one of those things. Testing is a necessary evil because you have to push the bikes to the limit, but there are risks involved. The factories have test riders but they can't do the job properly because they can't ride the bikes fast enough. The top riders are the only guys capable of putting in the speeds that the bikes will be ridden at in the races, and with the levels of refinement of these bikes, a couple of seconds a lap can be critical in assessing the machine. For example, when I tested the 1986 NSR500 at Surfers Paradise the bike behaved perfectly while we were doing consistent laps around the one-minute-thirteen-second mark. But when we dropped a second a lap, things started happening: it was understeering on fast corners and the suspension was bottoming out. There is such a fine line.

'Not that that was my problem at Surfers in 1987. The faster I got, the better the bike worked. The problem was that my mind started wandering after a couple of days. It's a funny thing when you get back on a race bike after a few months. It takes a while for your mind to adjust to the speed. You've slowed down to 100 kilometres per hour in the off-season while you're driving around the roads or whatever, and suddenly you're back doing 300 kilometres per hour. At first you get a big shock at the power, then after an hour or two back on the bike you get pretty blasé about it all—even though your mind might not have really caught up to the higher speeds yet. When I crashed I had just passed Mal Campbell, who was testing a Honda Australia Superbike at the time, and I turned around to wave to him. When l looked ahead again I had run out of track, and down I went. Bloody stupid, that's all it was, and it could have cost me dearly. As it was, the ankle injury was a nuisance but luckily it didn't really make much difference in the long run.'

Still, Gardner wasn't 100 per cent fit when he arrived at Suzuka Circuit for the opening round of the world championship. The race was enormously important for him. Obviously he wanted to get his title campaign off to a strong start, but there was much more to it than that. The world championship had returned to Japan for the first time in twenty years, and had generated enormous interest there. Honda owned Suzuka Circuit and were desperate for success. Gardner represented their best chance, despite the fact that Freddie Spencer was making a comeback after his disastrous, injury-riddled 1986 season. The Australian was the form rider at Suzuka, having won nine of his ten previous races there and it was virtually a home track to him, while most of the other GP riders had hardly raced there. The pressure to succeed was intense, fuelled by the presence of two film crews from Australia who were filming his every movement. One, from Australia's top-rating current affairs programme, 'Sixty Minutes', was filming a documentary which Gardner knew had the potential to make an enormous impact at home—for him personally and the whole image of motorcycle racing. He desperately wanted to succeed for 'Sixty Minutes'.

However, it wasn't to be, despite impressive qualifying form which saw him third on the grid behind Scot Niall MacKenzie, a surprise pole-sitter after one sizzling lap, and his old rival, Eddie Lawson. Rain bucketed down on the circuit just before the race, forcing the teams to change to wet-weather tyres and throwing qualifying form out the window. Randy Mamola ran away with the race on a Lucky Strike Yamaha shod with

Dunlop tyres, which were clearly superior in the wet to the Michelins that all the other major teams were using. Gardner rode a safe and steady race to finish second, which pleased him enough under the circumstances. But he was even more pleased when he heard the news that Lawson had pulled out of the race after making the wrong tyre choice and finding his machine unrideable. After just one race Gardner was twelve points up on the only rider he rated a serious threat to his own title hopes.

It was a promising start to the season and Gardner was elated. He was also determined to turn the screws even harder when the teams returned to Europe. The second round of the championship was at a new track at Jerez, in Spain, which hadn't been used for motorcycle GPs before. None of the riders knew Jerez, so the Rothmans Honda team booked it and spent Easter there, getting used to the twists and turns of the snaking racetrack. The work seemed to pay off during qualifying for the race, with Gardner dominating the early practice sessions. However, Lawson grabbed pole position with a late burst to pip Gardner by a third of a second.

The race was a completely different story. Lawson did take an early lead, but Gardner was climbing all over his rear wheel looking for a chance to pass him. By lap three he was through, and pulling away to an effortless twenty-four-second victory. 'When Eddie got away so well I just put my head down and thought "Right, you're not getting away from me",' Gardner recalls. 'But I soon realised he was actually holding me up, so on lap three I sighted an opening and ducked under him to take the lead.' Having done that, Gardner was determined to ram home his advantage. His lap boards were giving him a ten-second lead by the halfway point. Normally that would have been a signal to ease off and ride a bit more conservatively, to simply maintain the gap and make sure of finishing. However, Gardner was so confident that he decided to push even harder to completely demoralise Lawson and the Yamaha camp.

'If Eddie has a weakness, it is when he is under pressure,' Gardner says. 'If he thinks his machinery is equal to or better than yours, he is very, very hard to beat. But if he is worried about his bike, or thinks someone else's is faster, then he is more vulnerable. I tried to exploit that for all it was worth in 1987.

My bike really wasn't any better than the Yamahas, but I acted as though it was. It might have been marginally faster in the early races, but the Yamahas caught up. But I wanted Eddie to worry about my bike every time he went out, and to think the Honda was faster so that, whatever he did, I'd be able to pass him down the straight. It was a deliberate ploy, and I think I outsmarted him that season. He did a lot of moaning about how the Honda was so much better, but it wasn't really, although I let him believe it. He'd go into a race convinced the best he could do was come second. In qualifying all through that season I'd try to save my very best until just before the end of the final session, then try to put in a really fast lap to claim pole position when it was too late for the others to try to go faster.

'I'd be working at setting my bike up better and better in each of the four qualifying sessions. Towards the end of the final session I'd come in, rest for ten minutes and get new tyres fitted, then wait for a break in the traffic out on the track. Then I'd go out for two or three laps for the tyres to warm up, start to go hard in the fourth when the tyres were starting to break, then put in a really quick one on the fifth. Hopefully that would give me pole position, then I'd come in and hold a press conference and tell everyone that I had something in reserve, that I'd done just enough to get pole. I wanted the word to get back to Eddie and the other riders so they'd think they'd have no chance in the race. It didn't make me very popular. The Americans reckoned I was getting big-headed and they started slagging off at me to the press, but I didn't care. I was out there to win and it was a tactic designed to give me an advantage. If they didn't like it, too bad.' Gardner claimed pole position a stunning ten times in the fifteen-race season, often by as much as two seconds.

The West German Grand Prix at the ultra-fast Hockenheim Ring was the third round of the championship, and Gardner was absolutely awesome in qualifying on 2:04.27 seconds, an incredible five seconds under Freddie Spencer's old lap record. More importantly, though, he was two seconds ahead of the field, led by the Yamahas of Lawson and Christian Sarron. When the flag dropped Gardner inevitably went straight to the lead and began pulling away by a second a lap. It looked like a case of Gardner first, daylight second, when he was nine seconds ahead after just seven laps. Gardner could taste another victory coming up, but things quickly turned very sour. The electronics controlling the power valve in the exhaust system failed, effectively cutting the Honda's power by half. The valve was stuck in position for low revs, so there was plenty of drive out of corners, but once the revs climbed the engine would go flat. Gardner could do nothing as Lawson led the field past him.

'The power loss was dramatic—it felt like two cylinders had been disconnected. I hated seeing the guys go past but there was nothing I could do about it. I tried to keep up speed by riding harder through the corners but I had a few slides so I gave that up and just motored around, hoping to pick up a point or two,' Gardner explained later. He did that by finishing tenth to collect one point, whipping his ailing steed across the finish line like a jockey—much to the delight of the huge crowd in the amphitheatre-like grandstands that surround the final corner and home straight at Hockenheim. 'I might not have got the points I wanted at Hockenheim, but it was a moral victory. Eddie won the race but he knew it was a hollow win. I was speaking to him afterwards and asked him what he was planning to be doing in the three weeks before the next GP in Italy, and he said, "Looking for another twenty miles an hour." I knew that he was still worried about my bike.'

Monza in northern Italy is one of the most famous motor racing circuits in the world. It is also one of the fastest. Gardner looked tailor-made to win the fourth round of the championship when he took pole position one and a half seconds ahead of Lawson. This time there were no mechanical problems, and the blue-and-white Rothmans Honda streaked away to a commanding sixteen-second victory from Lawson and Sarron. However, the win wasn't as easy as it looked. There was drama aplenty behind the scenes, or at least behind the screen. Gardner had suffered a major nosebleed on the second lap, and each time he sat up into the wind to brake for a corner, blood was forced up his face into his eyes and across the screen of his helmet. It was potentially highly dangerous, and more faint-hearted riders may have pulled in. Not Gardner; he obliterated his rivals regardless. 'When I finished the race there was dried blood all over my face. Everyone got quite a shock when I took off my helmet.'

Gardner stretched his championship lead even further with successive victories in the next two GPs at Salzburg in Austria and Rijeka in Yugoslavia. Gardner dislikes the Salzburgring intensely. It is marvellous for spectators, with its great vantage points in a picture-postcard setting among the pine forests and alpine pastures, but its beauty belies its danger to the riders. The track is one of the fastest, with the most daunting section a 300-kilometre-per-hour uphill straight lined with armco fences lightly protected by hay bales. One mistake, hit that fence, and you could well be dead. It's as simple as that. Gardner, along with most of the other riders, would prefer not to race there. But each year it is retained on the calendar and he simply shrugs his shoulders and gets on with the job. In 1987 he rode one of the greatest races of his career there to win a fabulously exciting GP.

Lawson pulled out early with carburettor problems, but Randy Mamola proved a more-than-able opponent for Gardner, and the lead changed fourteen times as the two riders threw everything at each other. Twice their bikes collided as they were sucked into each other's slipstream on the long, fast uphill climb. Gardner finally got the better of his rival with some cool thinking and a liberal dash of racecraft. Over the concluding stages he slowed each time he came to the chicane leading onto the start/finish straight, hoping to lull Mamola into thinking that would be the place to pass on the final lap. Then, with two laps to go, he surprised the American by scorching through that section, and opening up enough of a break to win comfortably. In fact, Gardner set the fastest lap of the race and a new track record on the second-last lap as the plan took effect.

After the race, Gardner's first thought was to ring his parents in Wollongong—to apologise for scaring his father half to death. 'I knew Dad would be worried, watching a race like that on TV,' Gardner says. 'He knows Salzburg isn't the safest place, and to see me dicing with Randy like that must have been hard on him. I just wanted him to know that everything was under control and that I had felt quite safe.' As it happened, Norm Gardner had been unable to watch the race. He had been sick with worry all day at the prospect of his son racing at Salzburg, and when the race started he was pacing the hallway, while

Shirley Gardner yelled reports of their son's progress. Even that sort of information is now too stressful for Norm Gardner, and most races he leaves the house and waters his tomato plants or tinkers in the garage.

After six races Gardner had won four, finished second once, and picked up a point for tenth in a race he should have won. The championship seemed to be at his mercy, but for the next three rounds the wheels on his title bid, without exactly falling off, certainly wobbled a bit. He crushed his rivals in qualifying for the Dutch GP at Assen almost two seconds ahead, but finished second to Lawson in a rain-soaked race. Rain also drenched the French GP at Le Mans and this time Randy Mamola won while Gardner slipped and slithered his way to a disappointing fourth place. Then at Donington in the British GP a wrong tyre choice saw him powerless to hold off Lawson, and he finished second again after qualifying a second in front. In between the French and British GPs, he had made a lightning trip to Japan for the Suzuka Eight-hour, but the effort was wasted when co-rider Dominique Sarron crashed their Honda twice after they had held a one-and-a-half-lap lead at the halfway stage.

The pressure of leading the championship was beginning to take its toll. 'Sure, I was feeling the strain. It wasn't easy being in the lead, even though obviously I would rather have been fourteen points up than fourteen points down. There was a heavy expectation for me to keep winning and I was caught between riding for wins and going for points,' Gardner recalls. 'I guess I was pretty hard to live with.' That's a point with which Donna heartily concurs. She could see him getting more irritable and more tense as the pressure mounted, which is one of the reasons why she raised no objections when Gardner said he wanted to do the next race in Sweden on his own. The race at Anderstorp is traditionally a men-only affair. It's always run one week after the British GP and the teams and mechanics pack up their transporters and motorhomes and travel by car ferry to Sweden— with plenty of drinking, card-playing and general carousing on the way. As is so often the case, there was plenty of philosophising around that bar during the voyage, and Gardner arrived in Sweden with a new strategy for a race he simply had to win to reassert his authority on the championship and prevent his

Dining out with the flag marshalls—Austrian Grand Prix, Salzburg, 1988 (Nick Hartgerink)

'You must remember this . . .'
Wayne and Donna at the Japanese
Grand Prix, 1988 (Franco
Villani)

Very much at home in Monaco, June 1988 (Nick Hartgerink)

A Gardner Clothing modelling session with designer Kym Griffen and one of Wayne's vintage motorcycles—a 1923 Australian Waratah (Geoff Brown)

challenge disintegrating under the weight of self-doubt and negativism.

The Wollongong Kid made a comeback at Anderstorp. The larrikin Australian streak re-emerged through the tough veneer of control and coolness he had cultivated all season. Gardner went back to just being himself, a young guy out to have fun racing motorcycles. Gardner knew he had to win the race, so he applied himself as hard as ever during the qualifying sessions to finish on pole position once again. But after each day's practice he and the team would get together to relax over a few beers. Anderstorp is the sleepy backwater of GP racing, and there was little of the relentless television and press attention he had had to cope with at Donington. It was a welcome change.

'The lads thought I was getting too tense, that I was worrying too much about championship points and not enough about winning,' says Gardner. 'It was true. I was getting too caught up with riding safely, trying to be conservative so I wouldn't risk anything. They reckoned I needed to relax, so each night in Sweden we got together for a few beers. It seemed to work. By the Saturday I was jumping out of my skin. I really wanted to get out on the racetrack for the final session, and I couldn't wait for the race the next day.

'By Saturday night I was getting really pumped up about the race. I went back to the motorhome and turned a Bruce Springsteen tape up to full volume and marched up and down yelling and screaming along with the music. Anybody would have thought I had gone mad, but I was just getting mad. I kept yelling and telling myself I was going to go out there and thrash everyone the next day. Freddie Spencer's manager stuck his head inside the door looking for one of the Honda people, and got the shock of his life. He asked me if there was anything wrong, and I just told him to watch out, because no-one was going to get near me in the race. I was that pumped up I didn't care what I said.'

The next morning Gardner spent the few hours before the race alone in his motorhome, watching his favourite movie, *Top Gun*. The marvellous flying sequences also inspired him, so by the time he went out on the grid he was just about convinced he too could fly. When the flag dropped he rode a superb race, taking the lead on lap two and then spreadeagling the field to win easily from Lawson and Mamola. The Wollongong Kid celebrated with an exuberant wheelie for the length of Anderstorp's back straight. He had shown he was back on track for the world title. He knew it, and so did all his rivals. When he demolished the field from pole position at the next GP in Czechoslovakia he had raced twenty-six points clear. With a maximum of sixty points up for grabs in the final four races, it was obvious to all that desperate measures were called for if Gardner was to be denied the world championship.

CHAPTER 12

Cheap Tricks

The stakes are incredibly high in world championship motorcycle racing. It's a multi-million dollar sport and racetrack success translates into huge international bike sales for the manufacturers and vast promotional opportunities for the big tobacco companies that are the major sponsors. To the teams, success is everything, coming second is nothing. It's a situation that leads to desperation, and, as Gardner edged closer to the 1987 world title, he discovered just how desperate some of the rival teams were to throw him off-course.

After the Czechoslovakian Grand Prix, the riders headed to the Italian Adriatic coastal resort of Misano for the San Marino Grand Prix. Three days before the race the Italian press burst into print with a sensational story claiming that the world championship leader had big personal problems and his girlfriend had run off with a mechanic from another team. Donna had been seen without Wayne at the team transporter of West German 250-cc ace Toni Mang, and the rumours grew from there. By the time they burst into print, the reports claimed Donna went to visit her lover while Wayne was out riding his pushbike each morning. Gardner doesn't even have a pushbike, and Donna certainly doesn't have a lover. Forget the fact that Mang was also a Rothmans Honda rider, and that he and his wife Collette were close friends of Wayne and Donna. There was no substance at all to the rumour, but that didn't stop the story spreading like a bushfire, with each new burst of flame hotter and brighter than the previous one.

It even spread to Australia, being discussed on the television commentary of the live telecast of the race. Wayne and Donna were horrified and are convinced at least one rival team fanned the flames of the rumour to try to unsettle Gardner as much as possible for the race. It worked. Gardner rode poorly and struggled home a distant third behind Randy Mamola's Lucky Strike Yamaha and Eddie Lawson's Marlboro Yamaha. After the race he said the track simply didn't suit his Honda, but there was more to it than that. Gardner was deeply disturbed that he could be attacked through his personal life.

'It was incredible,' Gardner recalls. 'It was in the local Misano papers, and it even hit the headlines in the Italian national papers. We couldn't believe it. There were bits and pieces of stories flying all over the place—Donna going off with one of my mechanics, then with another team's mechanic. It just got bigger and bigger until it was like *Dynasty* all over again.' Donna says: 'The boss of Marlboro told us just to ignore it, that it had been done deliberately to upset Wayne.' The Marlboro man also told them that sort of thing happened all the time in Formula One car racing. If it was any consolation, at least it meant Gardner was now a star. That was indeed cold comfort, and the couple were furious and deeply upset, particularly over the hurt it would have caused their families and friends watching the telecast back home in Australia and wondering what was going on.

'I can't say for sure that any team actually set the whole thing up, but some of them certainly did manipulate it and spread it around. They just got wind of the situation and wound it up even more,' Gardner says. Donna still gets annoyed when she recalls the incident. 'Wayne called a press conference and got stuck right into the Italian journalists,' she recalls. 'He told them, "If you believe that, you're as silly as the journalist who wrote it," and they were all shocked. I was expected to catch the first plane out of the place but I just carried on as usual. I went out in pit lane when Wayne was practising the next day and no-one could believe it.' While Gardner may have been detuned by the publicity, he pulled himself together enough in the race to finish third and stay well in command in the championship chase. He was now even more acutely aware of just how high the stakes were, and it made him doubly determined to finish off the job. 'I haven't gone into my shell. I still plan to kick these guys' butts at least one more time this season,' he said after the race.

With three rounds of the world championship to go,

the pressure was intense when the teams went to Jarama in Spain for the last of the European races. After that they were to go for the first time to Brazil and Argentina, two unknown quantities for most of the riders. The Jarama race was actually the Portuguese Grand Prix, but it had been switched to Jarama because Portugal's Estoril Circuit had not been upgraded to the required safety levels. Gardner arrived at the scene of his first GP victory the year before, leading the championship by twenty-one points with 145 to Mamola's 124. Lawson was virtually out of the running on 115 and no-one else was even remotely close. A win here would virtually wrap up the title and Gardner was determined to do just that. The pressure on everyone was intense. Gardner was standing up to it but his Rothmans Honda let him down for the second time that season.

The race started well enough, with Gardner sitting just behind early leaders Lawson and Mamola. He looked something like an Aussie sheepdog bringing home two errant sheep as he hounded the two Yamaha riders, snapping at their heels and appearing to be in complete control. In those early laps Gardner set a new lap record and the race looked to be at his mercy. He was content to harry his rivals, confidently waiting for the chance to slip past and into the lead. However, by lap ten of the thirty-seven-lapper, his bike started losing power. A pinhole crack had formed in the radiator, and the engine pumped itself dry. As the coolant was lost, so the engine temperature soared and the power dropped. Two cylinders seized completely and it was a miracle that the bike kept going.

There was a further complication: the burning-hot coolant was spraying up over Gardner's leg and the heat coming up from his engine was burning through his leathers and gloves. The discomfort was extreme, but Gardner pressed on. He is not a quitter. He knew pulling out of the race would make his task of winning the world title a lot harder, so he gritted his teeth and rode on through the pain barrier. His reward was fourth place, and eight precious championship points—as well as bad blistering on his left hand and knee. 'The mechanics were amazed the bike had got home. They said it shouldn't have been running at all, and it would have only lasted a lap or two more before seizing up completely. I guess I was lucky in one respect, but all I felt was frustration. I could have wrapped up the title there and I really felt I could have won the race.'

After the Portuguese Grand Prix, Gardner spent what seemed like the longest fortnight of his life waiting to go to South America to discover whether his destiny was to be world champion. On the track Gardner may not have been getting much support from his fellow Honda riders against the Yamaha forces, but off the track the support was flooding in. People he'd never heard of sent messages urging him on. But more importantly, perhaps, his old friends were rallying to the cause. Roger Marshall rang from England to wish his old team-mate luck and to give some simple advice for the all-important Brazilian race: 'Don't hold back. Just go for it and you'll win for sure.' Barry Sisson, the other half of the partnership which had found the bike that started it all on the rubbish tip fourteen years earlier, dropped in to Monaco to wish Gardner well. Sisson was in Europe on holidays and made sure he got to Monaco before Gardner left for Brazil. And the phone line from Wollongong to Monaco rang hot as friends and family rang to voice their support. But one of Gardner's oldest friends went one better than everyone else. Roderick Summerville jumped on the first plane to South America. He'd known Gardner since they were toddlers, and had even organised the blind date on which Wayne met Donna. Whether Wayne won or lost in South America, Summerville wanted to be there. So there was no shortage of emotional support in the build-up to the most important race of Gardner's career. And on a practical level, the support came from one of the most experienced quarters in the game.

If Gardner's team had a weakness, it was the lack of a been-there/done-that former champion in the Giacomo Agostini or Kenny Roberts mould. While Mamola had Roberts at Lucky Strike, and Lawson had Agostini and Kel Carruthers at Marlboro Yamaha, the Rothmans Honda outfit didn't have a former champion calling the shots. But it did have Toni Mang, the thirty-seven-year-old West German 250-cc rider who had parcelled up his fifth world title at Jarama and was more than willing to guide Gardner through the difficult period leading up to the Brazilian GP.

'Toni was great value and I owe him a lot,' Gardner

says. 'I was pretty nervous as the race approached. Winning championships was nothing new to Toni and he was a great calming influence—just helping me keep my mind on the job and telling me not to worry, that somebody had to win so why not make sure it was me. He impressed on me the need to just keep on with the job I had been doing all year, not to do anything different or try anything new. It was really helpful having someone with his experience on my side.'

But Gardner was lucky to make it to the start line at Brazil. He had given his team an almighty fright when he ran off the track during qualifying, but managed to keep the Honda upright. 'I was catching Chili at the end of the straight, and wondering where to pass him. He isn't usually late on the brakes but he was this time, and while I was watching him I missed my braking marker and ran out of track. As I ran off the circuit I was thinking "Please don't crash, please don't crash" and somehow I managed to hold on to it. I was mightily relieved, I can tell you,' Gardner says. Honda Racing Corporation had left nothing to chance, shipping 1.5 tonnes of equipment to Goiania to make sure their star had the best possible support. He rewarded HRC with his ninth pole position of the season—almost a second ahead of Mamola. The American spread a story that Gardner was using special qualifying tyres and that things would be different in the race. He also predicted Gardner would go for a safe finish, leaving him and Lawson to fight it out for victory. It was a major miscalculation.

Gardner felt destiny was on his side. The world championship was within his grasp but he didn't want to win it by default—cruising around for a safe finish to collect the points. He wanted to win like a champion, with a smashing victory. Pole position was of no consequence if his bike wouldn't do the job in the race, so he worked hard all through qualifying to make sure the suspension was set up to handle the rough, bumpy surface. Nevertheless, Gardner was concerned with tyre wear in the scorching forty-degree heat. He settled on a race strategy of seeking to set up a big early lead, so he could nurse the tyres in the latter stages. The plan worked to perfection.

Lawson got the jump from the start and led the screaming pack to the first corner. But as he got there Gardner, much later on the brakes, forced his way past and into the lead. The message to the defending world champion couldn't have been clearer: 'Out of my way—this is my race and my world championship.' Gardner was one second ahead after the first lap, and simply ran away with the race from there. 'When I was eight seconds ahead at half-race distance I could afford to relax a little bit, but I was trying desperately not to think about the championship,' Gardner says. 'I was concentrating really hard on staying smooth and trying not to do anything stupid. For most of the race I managed to blot out the fact that I was riding for the world championship, but with two laps to go the whole thing hit me, and I realised I was just three minutes away from winning it. They were the longest two laps of my life and I did slow down a little because I was desperate for nothing to go wrong. That chequered flag was the best thing I had ever seen.' Gardner had won by more than five seconds from Lawson, with Mamola third. With one round of the championship to go he was twenty-two points ahead and couldn't be beaten.

Up on the rostrum, the new world champion wept unashamedly as the reality of his win hit home. Gardner's emotional flip-side—so different from the cool, calm image he tries so hard to project—had triumphed again. 'I was pretty much under control, until my team manager Jerry Burgess joined me on the rostrum and said, "Wayne, this is your day." That set off the tears, and when Donna came up too and gave me a hug and a kiss the tears just wouldn't stop. It was the realisation of a ten-year dream, all the hard work, all the frustrations . . . I couldn't quite believe that it was finally over, that I had done it. I had a funny empty feeling at first, like it had happened to someone else. But a day or two later it sank in, and I can tell you it felt great. In fact, it still does. I still think back to that day in Brazil. It was certainly one of the great moments in my life.'

Sadly, Lawson didn't come to the rostrum for the presentation and the crowning of the new champion who had just taken over his title. He said he had returned to his motorhome to change before the presentation, because of the extreme heat, and then had been refused access to the official area because the gateman hadn't recognised him without his leather racing suit on. Gardner was scornful of Lawson's non-appearance, seeing it as the act of a sore loser. 'I was disappointed,' he says. 'Eddie knows you go straight to the presentation in your leathers because all the sponsors like to have you up there on the rostrum with their logos on display. That was a pretty poor excuse. It looked to me as though he just couldn't accept that his title had gone.'

If Lawson was hurting, Gardner took great delight in rubbing salt into the wounds at the final race of the season in Buenos Aires on 4 October. Although he qualified in pole position, Gardner decided to use the race to experiment with some new Michelin tyres. The new rubber didn't really do the job, going off after four laps. Gardner relinquished his lead to Lawson, who looked as though he could at least salvage second place in the championship with a victory in the final race. But in the closing stages Gardner slowed and allowed Mamola through into second place, giving the Lucky Strike man enough points to pip Lawson by just one for the right to the number-two plate in 1988. The final championship points saw Gardner on 178 followed by Mamola on 158 and Lawson on 157. 'I can't say I was too disappointed to see Eddie pipped like that,' Gardner says. 'I was pretty dirty on him for a few things he had said about me during the season, and all the bitching that had gone on, so it was a good result for Randy to get up there for second in the championship. He deserved it, anyway.'

It had been a magnificent season for Gardner—fifteen races, seven victories, ten pole positions and ten new lap records. The racing over, Gardner headed home to Australia to savour the sweet taste of victory.

CHAPTER 13

All-Australian Hero

When Wayne Gardner left Australia in March 1981 he was a nobody, but when he returned in October 1987 as the newly crowned world champion he was definitely a somebody. He was Australia's latest sporting hero, and he received a rapturous welcome. Every country loves a winner, and Australians are no different. Never mind that a few short years before, most Australians had considered motorcycle racing was just for a few crazies with a death wish, watched by drunken, leather-clad Hell's Angels. Now they knew differently, thanks to Gardner; and everyone from the Prime Minister down queued to congratulate the country's first 500-cc world champion.

Wayne and Donna flew into Sydney from Japan early on the morning of Saturday 17 October. They had been warned to expect a big welcome, but nothing could have prepared them for what lay ahead. Hundreds of fans and a huge media contingent greeted them at Sydney airport, but the real welcome was planned for Wollongong. Their proud home town had been preparing all week to turn on a homecoming fit for a hero, and the Wollongong Lord Mayoral limousine was despatched to Sydney airport to collect them. It was escorted by police motorcyclists and scores of other riders for the eighty kilometres to Wollongong, where the motorcade halted at the top of the escarpment overlooking the city so that Wayne and Donna could transfer to an open car—fittingly a Honda Prelude convertible—for the drive into town.

Rain began to fall as the car descended Bulli Pass to Wollongong's northern suburbs, drenching Wayne and Donna, but they were warmed by the sight that greeted them. Along the twenty-kilometre route into the city the highway was lined with people all waving and cheering. The Bulli fire station bell was ringing and the firemen were lined up outside to doff their helmets at the passing parade. Coal trucks and family sedans alike honked their horns, and a florist ran from her shop to hand out red roses. Gardner was stunned by the number of people who had braved the rain, but he was even more flabbergasted when the motorcade arrived at Wollongong's central shopping mall. There a crowd of more than 10,000 had gathered to pay homage to their hero. They roared with delight as his car, festooned with streamers, edged its way through the crowd towards the stage. Appropriately, the sun broke through the clouds as the car entered the mall, bathing the crowd in bright sunshine. 'This is the greatest day of my life,' Gardner told the multitude. 'The day I won the world championship in Brazil was special, but nothing compares with this. I am completely overwhelmed by how many people are here. I knew some kind of welcome was planned but never in my wildest dreams could I have anticipated something like this. It is amazing and I am very touched. I am ever so proud to be back home and ever so proud of this huge welcome. All I can say is thank you.' Then the Gardner emotion took over. His voice cracked and the tears flowed. The crowd loved him for it, and cheered even louder. It was a very special moment for all who were there, especially Gardner, and he still says it is one of his most treasured memories.

Nine television crews and more than thirty journalists and photographers covered the event, which was shown on every television news program that night and on other television shows around Australia for days afterwards. The media spotlight was pointed straight at Gardner, and it burned brightly all summer. It seemed the media's appetite for him was insatiable. Australian Associated Press sports editor Bill Allen describes the Gardner phenomenon thus: 'It was incredible. Nobody had heard of him and then he was a superstar. Whenever we sent a story out across Australia [on the AAP wire service] it would get picked up by just about everyone. There are not too many people in that category.' Gardner recognised his responsibilities to promote his sport and didn't shirk them. He was delighted that, at last, motorcycle racing was considered a mainstream sport worthy of mass media attention and he recognised he had to capitalise on that. He agreed whenever humanly possible to requests for television, radio and newspaper interviews. From October until mid-February he had just seven days when he didn't have at least one media commitment—and that included Christmas Day and a few days on a secluded Barrier Reef island (to where Donna, in her desperation to give him at least a few days off, had made Wayne flee). Even then, the local North Queensland media heard of the couple's whereabouts and were waiting for them when they returned to the mainland.

But that wasn't all. Politicians, ever eager to fete a winner, got into the act as well. A State reception in Gardner's honour was hosted by the New South Wales premier and he had lunch at the national Parliament in Canberra with senior government ministers. The irony wasn't lost on Gardner. 'Back in 1981 I had applied for a sporting assistance grant to help me get overseas to race. It was only five thousand but the government said I didn't deserve it, and gave the money to some tennis players. And here they were having me to lunch,' he says with a laugh.

Australia was in the midst of its Bicentennial celebrations that summer and Wayne and Donna received invitations to every major function. They breakfasted with the Prime Minister at his residence on the shores of Sydney Harbour on Australia Day, and Gardner was one of the stars at a Royal concert in front of the Prince and Princess of Wales. Appearing before Royalty might be enough to frighten the most experienced performer, but not the Wollongong Kid. In fact, he almost missed his cue. The concert was conceived as a Bicentennial extravaganza, celebrating 200 years of Australian cultural and sporting achievements. Gardner was billed as 'the hero of our time' and was scheduled to ride his bike onto the stage and do a lap of honour. However, just thirty minutes before he was due to appear, he was stuck in the middle of Sydney Harbour on a Spanish 'tall ship' which was to take part in a Bicentennial sail-past the next day.

'I'd been invited out on the ship for the afternoon, and the captain assured me we would be back at the wharf by 5 p.m.,' Gardner recalls. 'But the harbour was really congested and we couldn't get back in. By seven o'clock I was panicking because I knew I had to be on stage in half an hour. We flagged down a police launch which took me to the nearest wharf, then I ran three kilometres up to the Sydney Entertainment Centre. I rushed into the dressing-room just as they were trying to shoehorn a rather large stagehand into my leather racing suit to take my place. I had made it with just a minute or two to spare. Imagine being late for Princess Di—that would have been madness!' A week later Prince Charles and Princess Diana were in Wollongong to open a new Performing Arts Centre, but the few thousand who turned out to welcome them paled against the throng that had attended Gardner's homecoming. And the crowd at the Performing Arts Centre gave a bigger cheer to Gardner than to the Royals when he and Donna arrived at the centre as guests for the function. Wollongong now had its own 'Royal Couple', and were mighty proud of them.

There was plenty more fun. Gardner was invited to Adelaide for the Australian Formula One Grand Prix to perform a lap of honour in front of 100,000 appreciative fans. While there, he went flying with the Royal Australian Airforce aerobatics squadron, the Roulettes. Gardner loved his day with the airforce, and challenged them to a standing quarter-mile 'drag race' down a runway, between his motorcycle and an FA-18 Hornet jet fighter. The Hornet won, then Gardner was taken for a flight in one of the most sophisticated jet fighters in the world. He even had a stint at the controls, with the pilot keeping a watchful eye on proceedings.

As a fitting climax to a great year, Gardner won the two major annual awards for sportsmen—the Confederation of Australian Sport's Male Athlete of the Year and the ABC Sportsman of the Year. He had beaten tennis star Pat Cash, who had won Wimbledon that year, golfing superstar Greg Norman and world champion boxer Jeff Fenech. Gardner, and motorcycle racing, had arrived at last.

While Gardner is obviously fast on the track, he is also not slow to recognise opportunities off it. Clearly, his fame in Australia provided the chance to add to his fortune. Honda Australia, after years of unexplained indifference to Gardner, finally recognised his promotional potential and used him in major advertising pushes for the Honda CRX car and its range of motor scooters. Gardner had been keen to interest a major Australian company in personal sponsorship for some years, and Alan Bond's

Swan brewery was the first to recognise his value. Swan signed up early in the 1987 season for a substantial six-figure annual sum over three years. The contract gave Swan the right to use Gardner in international marketing, and to have its logo on his leathers and helmet. Swan also produced a magnificent television commercial based on the theme 'They Said You'd Never Make It', which followed Gardner's struggle from his first bike through to Grand Prix glory. The commercial further promoted Gardner's image and profile across Australia. It put him on the same lofty pedestal as Greg Norman and America's Cup-winning yacht designer Ben Lexcen, who had also featured in the campaign. Since linking with Gardner, Swan has become increasingly committed to supporting motorcycle sport. The brewery is sponsoring the Phillip Island Grand Prix to the tune of five million dollars over three years.

The Swan connection also led Gardner into the clothing trade. For some years he had toyed with the idea of a clothing label with a range somewhat more upmarket than the motor sport staples of T-shirts and sweatshirts. While filming the Swan commercial in 1987, he met Kym Griffen, an artistic director with the advertising company making the ads. They discussed Gardner's ideas, and Griffen turned them into concepts. Jessica Bokey, who operates a Sydney fashion house, turned the concepts into garments, and a new label was born. Gardner Clothing is now available at major retailers across Australia, and is also breaking into the potentially enormous Japanese market. The range includes shirts, jackets, polo shirts and track pants, and it is firmly pitched in price and quality at the top end of the leisure-wear market. And obviously there is a perfect medium for promoting it: whenever Gardner appears on television wearing the latest garment, demand surges for that garment. 'I always had an idea I'd like to be involved in fashion,' Gardner says. 'I had a couple of approaches from companies but nothing really grabbed me. My family company had a good range of T-shirts and so on, but I wanted something really different, away from the motorcycle theme. Not everyone wants to have a motorcycle blazed across their chest. And I wanted to be able to wear my own gear for television appearances and so on, but sometimes it just wasn't appropriate to turn up in a T-shirt.' Griffen says

Gardner Clothing is pitched at three main markets in Australia: 'First, there's the Gardner fan who is prepared to spend more money on a quality product that won't fall apart,' Griffen says. Then there's any fashion-conscious person who simply likes the look of the gear because it is different and distinctive, but doesn't shout "Gardner the Hero" across the front. Finally, I think there is a real market for Japanese tourists visiting Australia who are Gardner fans.'

Gardner has seen other possibilities with Japanese tourists. He and an old school friend, Terry Looney, who runs a travel business, have established Wayne Gardner's Australian Tours. Together, they bring groups of Japanese bike enthusiasts to Australia, equip them with motorcycles and a tour guide, and let them loose on Australia's vast road network. The highlight of the trip comes when Gardner joins the tour for a few days, but as he spends little time in Australia the tours are available only for a few months a year.

Behind all this is Wayne Gardner Enterprises, the family company run by his parents and sister Vicki. It started back in 1982, when Gardner told his father he'd bought a truckload of motorcycle brake pads and was shipping them to Australia. Norm Gardner gave up driving trucks to set up a business to sell the brake pads and establish something for his son to fall back on if his racing career didn't flourish as anticipated. Wayne's racing did flourish, and so did the business. Today it is a thriving operation employing six staff and distributing European Brake Corporation brake pads and clutches, and a range of Gardner's racing gear, including racing replica Shoei helmets, signature Gaerne riding boots and a wide range of Rothmans Honda jackets and T-shirts.

Gardner and his manager Harris Barnett have other interests around the world, including a share in a motorcycle dealership in London, but it isn't a subject he likes talking about. 'Let's just say Harris and I have some investments. We're pretty careful about what we put my money into. There are always people trying to convince us of the value of this project or that, but we don't need to take any risks. I leave that side of things to Harris—if he's not entirely satisfied then we don't do it, it's as simple as that. And Harris is a pretty hard man to convince.

I know of quite a few sportsmen who have made a lot of money and had a fair bit of it go down the drain by getting involved in silly schemes. I'm not about to let that happen to me.'

Gardner and his sports pyschologist Phil Fearon. They joined forces at the end of 1985 (Nick Hartgerink)

Manager Harris Barnett, Donna, Wayne, and good friend Roger Marshall at the Dutch Grand Prix, June 1986 (Nick Hartgerink)

Best of friends since their Moriwaki days in 1981—Wayne and Roger Marshall in Holland, June 1986 (Nick Hartgerink)

Mutual Admiration Society—Gardner and 'King' Kenny Roberts, who tried to sign him for Lucky Strike Yamaha in 1986 and 1987 (Nick Hartgerink)

Dressing up for the Japanese fans—Suzuka Circuit, March 1987 (Nick Hartgerink)

'Hey, it's good to be back home.' Wayne and Donna, Sydney Airport, September 1986 (Illawarra Mercury)

Wayne just can't slow down, even during the off-season (Illawarra Mercury)

'Where is everyone?' Wayne's world championship year, 1987 (Rothmans Press Service)

Next best to the real thing. Parents Norm and Shirl and sister Vicki toast a cardboard cut-out of Gardner the day he won the 1987 world championship with victory in the Brazilian Grand Prix (Illawarra Mercury)

Wollongong welcomes home its world champion, October 1987 (Hank van Stuivenberg)

Two high fliers—Wayne gives an FA18 Hornet a drag race at Williamtown RAAF base, February 1988 (Gardner Collection)

Wayne and Donna meet the Prince and Princess of Wales in Wollongong, February, 1988 (Hank van Stuivenberg)

Crocodile Wayne, as the French press dubbed him, with his Akubra hat. Yugoslavia, July 1988
(Rothmans Press Service)

Honda's two number ones—arch rivals Wayne Gardner and Eddie Lawson. Phillip Island, February 1989 (Australian Grand Prix Press Picture)

Gardner and long-time mentor Mamoru Moriwaki plot tactics before the 1989 Japanese Grand Prix (Nick Hartgerink)

Working out to prepare for a long, hard season, Wollongong, February 1989 (Illawarra Mercury)

Rothmans Honda's 1989 team (from left)—Eddie Lawson, Wayne Gardner and Michael Doohan, Phillip Island, April 1989 (Rothmans Press Service)

Pit Lane mayhem at the Australian Grand Prix, Phillip Island, April 1989 (Peter Geran)

German backmarker Michael Rudroff brings down Wayne Gardner during practice for the Australian Grand Prix, Phillip Island, April 1989 (Series by Patrick Gosling)

Wayne and Donna share a drink with Scottish rider Niall MacKenzie and his girlfriend Jan Burtenshaw in Wollongong, April 1989 (Illawarra Mercury)

Gardner interviewed for television by former world champion Barry Sheene at the Australian Grand Prix, Phillip Island, April 1989 (Nick Hartgerink)

Donna hitches a ride with Wayne at Phillip Island, April 1989 (Nick Hartgerink)

Stuck in the mud—Gardner with his friend, Japanese rider Shunji Yatsushiro have some fun motocrossing in Wollongong, February 1989 (Illawarra Mercury)

Broken leg, broken dreams—Wayne and Donna after the accident which ended his 1989 world championship hopes (Mike Kable)

CHAPTER 14

The Price of Fame

Fame sneaked up on Wayne Gardner. He started building an overseas following in 1981 in Britain and Japan. As his career blossomed, so did the number of his fans. By 1985 he was an established Grand Prix star and the Japanese fans, in particular, took him to their hearts. It was next to impossible for him to move anywhere in the vicinity of Suzuka Circuit without being mobbed. Girls slept outside his hotel-room door, others wept if he didn't win. Flying back to Europe from Tokyo after winning the 1985 Suzuka Eight-hour race, his plane stopped at Anchorage, Alaska. In the terminal, much to the amazement of airport staff, he was besieged by a hundred or so Japanese schoolgirls on their way to the United States for a sporting visit. After all, he had just won one of Japan's biggest sporting events—a race that attracts a staggering 700 media representatives from Japan alone, and massive television coverage across the country. And while his star shone brightest in Japan, in Europe Gardner was also learning to deal with the constant demands of sporting stardom, especially at the racetracks where there is never a moment's peace for the leading riders.

In Australia, fame came more slowly. His mother Shirley would receive more fan mail from East Germany and Czechoslovakia than from Australia. It wasn't until he started winning GPs in 1986 that the Australian mass media, and thus the public, started taking notice of Gardner. That success generated delayed telecasts of the GPs, and then live coverage of each race in 1987 as Gardner won the world championship. His fame was spreading. In the inaugural Australian Grand Prix at Phillip Island in April 1989, victory, especially in such an exciting race, pushed him into the superstar league. It was front page news in every major newspaper across the country, and thousands of fan letters poured into the family business. One fan letter even came from the Prime Minister, Bob Hawke, who said, 'Congratulations Wayne on such a wonderful win in yesterday's first Australian Motorcycle Grand Prix. Spectators at the track echoed the delight of all Australians at your hard-fought victory in front of your home crowd. A thrilling performance which augurs well for your chances of regaining the world championship this year. Continued good luck in the future.'

If any further proof is needed, now an Australian film company is producing for Australian and international release a four-hour television mini-series based on Gardner's career. The budget is more than five million dollars and an all-star cast will play the leading roles. In fact, it is easy to argue that Gardner's success led directly to the establishment of a multi-million-dollar industry based around televising GPs from overseas and to the staging and promoting of the Australian Grand Prix.

Gardner still can't quite believe it has happened to him in Australia—a country he left as a complete unknown in 1981. 'I come back to Australia only for a couple of months each year, and every time I come home I get a shock at how the whole thing has grown, and how it keeps growing. It's only just starting to sink in for me now—I'm a big hero with Aussie kids and, funnily enough, older people as well. I really never thought it would get to this stage. I thought people would always see motorcyclists as bikies in leather jackets—that we could never change the image. But it has changed—imagine, a motorcycle racer going to breakfast with the Prime Minister, and being late of course! Or having a mini-series made about my life. And now, when I go to a television station, the personalities greet me like a long-lost friend, even if I've never met them before. It's all a bit hard to believe sometimes.'

Wayne and Donna needed quite a lot of convincing before agreeing to the mini-series proposal. Melbourne-based film company Simpson le Mesurier Films approached Gardner in mid-1988 with the idea, but it wasn't until November of that year that they agreed to it. 'It was a difficult thing to come to terms with for Donna and me, even though it was a great honour to think a film company would consider it worthwhile doing a series on my life. I thought that only happened to famous dead people,' Wayne says. 'Obviously they weren't going to just make a TV show about the racetrack, there would be a lot of personal stuff in it as well. It was a matter of deciding whether we were prepared to have our private lives on public display. In the end we agreed to it because we could see a lot of benefits, for me personally and for motorcycle racing, and we were intrigued to see how it would turn out. But it will be very strange sitting down to watch it.' Producer Roger Simpson said Gardner's life story couldn't help but make exciting television: 'It's a real story about a real hero—about a guy who found a motorcycle on a rubbish tip when he was thirteen, had a dream of making it to the top and got there through sheer determination. It's a story with danger, drama, romance, a battle against the odds—everything you need for a good TV show—and it's true. As a bonus, it's set in the exciting world of Grand Prix motorcycle racing, which makes a great story even better.' The mini-series is due for completion and screening around the world in 1990.

Perhaps the most surprising aspect of Gardner's fame and popularity in Australia is that he has been able to maintain it. The 'tall poppy syndrome' flourishes in Australia, where achievers are pushed up just far enough to have their heads lopped off by an ever-critical public and media. Even a hint of big-headedness or conceit is enough to turn public opinion against you, as many sportspeople have found to their cost. Through all his success, and his rise from unemployed boilermaker to multi-millionaire superstar, Gardner has managed to retain his boy-next-door image as an ordinary Aussie guy. And it's true. He still likes to come back to Wollongong, pack up the car and head off down the coast water-skiing with his mates—just as he might have done each weekend if he'd stayed working at Tubemakers.

Gardner enjoys the fame, even if there is a hefty price to pay for the dramatic change in his life and lifestyle since 1981. 'Your life changes in a few ways. You can afford nice things such as boats and cars and a much more pleasurable lifestyle,' he says. Gardner's list of 'toys' in Monaco includes a recently acquired Ferrari Testerossa (which replaced a Mercedes 560SEC), a Golf Cabriolet for negotiating the narrow, winding streets, and the pièce de résistance, a forty-seven-foot Sunseeker luxury speed cruiser with twin 700-horsepower diesel engines. There's even an 883-cc Harley-Davidson Sportster and a couple of Honda scooters which Wayne and Donna use to go down to the beach. In Wollongong he keeps a ski boat, with a Range Rover to haul it, a Honda CRX for Donna to drive, and a Honda VFR750 road bike.

'Look, I'd be kidding if I said I didn't like being able to afford all these things. It's great, but you've also got to work for it too. You're public property. You can't do a lot of things because of who you are, and what people might think if they see you,' Gardner says. 'I'm owned by the public in some ways and I have to watch everything I do. If I'm out on a training run and I'm desperate for a pee, I can't stop and do it in the bushes like some other runner might do. Another thing I can't do is go to the pub for a few quiet drinks alone with friends. The drunks come up and want to talk about racing. And of course they all want to tell me how I can improve my bike, or what I should have done to win a particular race, or to ask me what I really think of Eddie Lawson. You can't be rude, because they mean well, and after all it is the paying public that keeps me in a job. You've got to be nice to everyone, even if you're mad or angry or something.'

Like one night during practice for the Australian Grand Prix. Gardner had been out at the track at seven that morning for the first television interview, then had done several more during the day, as well as press conferences and all sorts of other media work. And in between that he'd squeezed in two practice sessions. 'That night I was just knackered, and I'd certainly had enough of people,' Gardner recalls. 'A group of us went out for a quiet meal and I ended up spending the night signing autographs and talking to people who came up to our table. It was hard to keep smiling because I was absolutely exhausted—but if you show some human feelings and just say "Please leave me alone", you're the worst person in the world. In the end I had to say I'd had enough, and I guess some people went away disappointed and thinking I'd done the wrong thing. But what could I do? I'd just had enough. You've got to work at it seven days a week, twenty-four hours a day. That's the worst part about being famous. There's no free time and there's nowhere you can go without being noticed. But on the other hand it's nice to be recognised and appreciated for what you do—especially by the kids. I love that side of it.'

There is one haven to where Gardner can escape. Monaco is his refuge from the pressures and demands of superstardom. This pricey principality nestling under the mountains on France's Mediterranean coast has been his home since early 1987 and it's the one place where he can get away from the demands of his job. There he can eat at a restaurant without signing a dozen menu cards, lie on the beach without being interviewed or photographed, or ride his motor scooter around the twisting streets without having his braking technique analysed and written about in a dozen journals. While most people go to Monaco looking for excitement at the casino or ritzy nightclubs, Gardner goes there looking for peace—and anonymity. 'Monaco is very important for me,' he says. 'Nobody worries who you are or what you do. They just do their own thing and leave you to do yours. It's a nice change, because at the racetrack I get absolutely no privacy, and I go back to Monaco between races to get away from it all,' he says.

But that is only one of the reasons Gardner sought resident status in Monaco. The tax advantages enjoyed by Monaco residents had not gone unnoticed by Gardner or Harris Barnett. And its location is ideal. 'Donna and I had our house in Wragby in Lincolnshire from 1982, and we loved living in England. But when I started racing GPs full-time we hardly ever used it. In 1986 I think we went back to Wragby for a total of three weeks in the whole season. It just took too much time to fly back to England then drive up from London to Lincolnshire. And it was even worse if we were driving across Europe and then waiting for Channel ferries and that kind of thing. It got to a stage where we had to look for something a bit more practical and Monaco seemed perfect. It was pretty central, with races along the Mediterranean countries in France, Spain, Portugal, Italy and Yugoslavia, and good transport routes by road or air to the other major European circuits. Besides, the climate is great and it's right on the beach.' Just the thing for the Wollongong Kid.

Donna well remembers her first experience of Monaco. 'I wasn't particularly keen on the move at first because I liked living in England,' she says. 'And Wayne painted a really gloomy picture of the whole thing. He told me apartments were so hard to come by that he'd had to settle for a dingy room with cracking

111

plaster and a naked light bulb swinging from the ceiling. I didn't know what to expect when we got there, but he was only pulling my leg. He and Harris had actually found a beautiful apartment with great views over the harbour and the palace. And we love the life there now. It's just about the only place we can be ourselves and not have to worry about what other people think of us. And it is good for Wayne to get a break from the pressures and all the attention.'

The other side of the fame picture is that Gardner has devoted almost as much time and energy to developing his media talents as to his riding talents. So if he doesn't like the attention, he has himself to blame. Back in 1980 the sight of a television interviewer heading his way with a microphone would strike more fear into his heart than running out of brakes at the end of a 280-kilometre-per-hour straight. But, with the help of Peter Molloy and later Barry Symmonds at Honda Britain, he recognised that the publicity side of motorcycle racing was almost as important as the racing. If he was good at PR, he would be more valuable for his sponsors and thus could attract fatter contracts. Gardner has worked hard on it ever since, developing a natural openness and humour that make him an ideal talk show guest. His credits include appearances with Britain's most popular chat show host, Terry Wogan, and he is greatly sought after by Australia's most popular television shows whenever he is the country. And while some so-called stars charge hefty fees to appear on television programmes or conduct interviews, Gardner's policy has always been that it is part of his job, and one of the reasons why his sponsors pay so well to be associated with him.

Gardner is well known amongst the international motorcycle press contingent for accessibility and frankness. BBC commentator and freelance journalist Nick Harris believes Gardner is one of the best media performers he has observed in a long association with the sport. 'The thing about Wayne is that he'll give you an honest answer. He recognises the role the media plays and works in with us as much as he can—certainly a lot more than most riders. And it is his honesty that has the most appeal. It means you'll always get a quotable quote from Wayne,' Harris says. Gardner does try hard to be available to the media at the racetrack. He holds regular press conferences and does countless interviews on the run. It is something he is proud of, because he feels the leading riders owe it to the sport to promote it as much as possible. But he was deeply hurt and angered at the end of 1988 when French magazine *Moto Journal* published a poll alleging that European journalists had voted him the least co-operative rider on the circuit. Perhaps not surprisingly, a French rider, Dominique Sarron, topped the poll. It was scorned by most English-speaking journalists as a bad joke, but nevertheless Gardner was furious. 'What a bunch of bastards,' he says. 'They all turned up at my press conferences and fed off what I had to say. I'd try hard to meet any reasonable demand, and then they turned on me like that. They didn't even have the decency to put their names to it. I felt very let down after all the work I'd put into making myself accessible.'

Gardner has mixed feelings about the international press contingent that follows the teams from track to track. 'Most of them are really good and understanding, but some are complete ratbags,' he says. 'Some of them are completely unprofessional. They talk about the teams and riders being unprofessional, but I think sometimes they should look at themselves and start being a bit more professional in the things they write. They twist things and sometimes they just make things up. Everyone—the riders, the teams—is trying to improve the whole package of motorcycle racing as a travelling show, but sometimes the press don't play their part. For example, if you can't do something for them because you've got other commitments, they'll get a set against you and write bad things about how you're not prepared to be interviewed or whatever. And of course they're always heavily biased towards the riders from their own country—like the *Moto Journal* poll. That really showed how two-faced they are, because there was never any suggestion that they were having any trouble getting me to co-operate, until that came out in the magazine. They forced me to change my attitude to the media. Now I organise a time and tell them I'll give them twenty minutes and that's it. I tried to win the publicity stakes by being a little bit more friendly and more accessible, but it made no difference, so from the beginning of the 1989 season I decided to go the opposite way and make it a bit more difficult for them—make them appreciate the time I do give them.'

Gardner passionately believes that the reigning world champion has a responsibility to promote the sport. 'We make a lot of money out of racing, and it is our responsibility to put something back into it—to make it better and more widely publicised. We've also got a real duty to promote the image of racing. It had a bad image in Australia a few years ago because of some trouble at the annual Easter bike races at Bathurst. The public saw it as a place where bikies went to fight with the police. But in Europe it is so different—it's a real enthusiasts' sport with lots of family involvement. I tried very hard to get that message across in Australia and I think it has worked. You only have to look at the type of people who went to Phillip Island for our first GP. There were 100,000 people on the island for the weekend and there was no trouble. It was fantastic, and I was very proud of everyone who went there—proud of Australia.'

Gardner's victory in the 1987 world championship, and the blaze of publicity that surrounded it, gave him the perfect opportunity to promote motorcycle racing to a most receptive Australian public. Gardner certainly didn't shirk his responsibility in the Australian summer after his victory, and his work continued all the next year while he carried the number-one plate on his bike.

Despite the pressures on his time, Gardner has never lost touch with the ordinary people who make the sport tick. The 1988 Austrian Grand Prix at Salzburg is a classic example. A trackside barbecue with a group of complete strangers is just about the last way you'd think a world champion would spend the night before one of his most important races of the year. But that's what Gardner did on the eve of the Austrian GP— a race he had to win if he was to have any chance of retaining his title. After final practice on the Saturday evening, when the other riders had closeted themselves away in motorhomes or hotel suites with their minders to plot their strategies for the next day's racing, Gardner was learning the finer points of serving radish Austrian-style.

He and Donna were being plied with enormous glasses of beer and being force-fed spicy sausage cooked on a tiny charcoal barbecue and smothered with mustard. There were five Austrians sitting around the table. Gardner didn't know any of them, but they all knew him and were clearly greatly honoured to have the reigning world 500-cc champion 'dine' with them. They were the flag marshals, those volunteers who are the backbone of motorcycle racing. They man the racing circuits for four days of anything from searing heat to pouring rain, ready to leap into action with their flags to warn following riders if there is a fall or some other obstacle on the track. The marshals play a vital safety role but rarely, if ever, do they see more than a fleeting glimpse of the riders they protect. These particular marshals had seen Wayne and Donna working with a photographer on the track, and insisted they join their barbecue. Wayne and Donna were happy to oblige, and spent half an hour eating, drinking and laughing with their hosts, not to mention learning something of culinary art.

Gardner sees such activities as the pleasant duty of a world champion, and he is highly critical of Eddie Lawson's approach. The quiet Californian is totally different from the outgoing Australian. Where Gardner wears his heart on his sleeve, Lawson rarely displays emotion and spends as little time as possible in the public gaze. 'Eddie's a bad world champion,' Gardner says. 'I can't understand and I can't justify his attitude sometimes. He's totally strange to the point where he gets off the bike and shuts the door. He doesn't promote himself and he doesn't help motorcycle racing. A good champion would be out publicly promoting the sport. But Eddie just wins then goes away and locks himself in the house and you don't see him any more. And he doesn't turn up at press conferences, although that did improve a bit when he joined the Rothmans Honda team.'

By his own definition, Gardner considers himself a good world champion. Certainly, he devoted himself to the task of promoting the sport after he had won the title in 1987. But ironically, it was this effort which probably cost him any chance of successfully defending the world title. The punishing schedule Gardner imposed on himself from late 1987 to early 1988 meant he arrived at pre-season testing in February completely exhausted. It was not exactly the ideal preparation for a long, wearying campaign to retain the title. He and his team allocated just a few days in February to test the new Honda NSR500 racing bike—not nearly enough time to detect some of the faults that were being built into the new bike. He didn't realise it that February, but 1988 was shaping as a disaster.

CHAPTER 15

Looking After Number One

Winning a world championship may be hard, but defending it is even harder. In 500-cc motorcycle racing, no rider had successfully defended his title since 'King' Kenny Roberts won three straight from 1978 to 1980. Some great riders had tried, but all had failed. There seemed to be one reason for this: the winning factory rested on its laurels, unwilling to alter a winning machine, while the losers tried doubly hard in the off-season to improve their bikes. Wayne Gardner planned to change all that, and he arrived in Japan for the first race of the 1988 season supremely proud at last to be carrying the number-one plate on his bike, and convinced he could hold on to it. He was even setting his sights on winning three straight to cement his name in history as Roberts had done.

Gardner knew it would not be easy, and he had recalled sports psychologist Phil Fearon to help him adjust to the demands of being a champion. Suddenly, from being one of the hunters, he was now the hunted, pursued by a pack of good riders who had him firmly in their sights. And as world champion, he faced responsibilities that he had not experienced before. He was the spearhead of his sport, spokesman for the riders, and the centre of the media's attention. Three nights before the Japanese GP he took his team for a beer to the famous riders' haunt, Mumma's Bar, in downtown Suzuka City. Although he hardly touched a drink, the next day the press room was full of stories about how Gardner was turning to alcohol to help him handle the pressure. And the ever-attentive Japanese fans didn't give him any peace. The night before the race, he had to be smuggled down the fire escape in pop-star fashion at the Suzuka Circuit Hotel when hundreds of fans jammed the foyer clamouring for his autograph.

However, his optimism about a successful title defence

seemed well placed. After all, he had finished the 1987 season in dominant style, and could see no reason why that shouldn't continue. Although the team had hardly done any testing, they had worked on problem areas from the previous season—such as the brakes. Honda had beefed up the brakes and Gardner was very pleased with the results during the few days spent testing the bike at Calder Raceway in Melbourne. However, Calder is nothing like a Grand Prix circuit, and the testing there failed to show up a fundamental flaw that had been built into the new NSR500. A change of design staff at Honda Racing Corporation had brought some fresh ideas, and the steering geometry and frame on the 1988 bike were quite different from the '87 bike. Even the Japanese Grand Prix qualifying sessions at Suzuka failed to indicate the trouble ahead, and Gardner claimed his usual position on the front row of the grid. But his season almost ended before it really started.

Gardner and Suzuki's new star, lanky Texan Kevin Schwantz, made the Japanese Grand Prix their own. The pair sprinted away from the field and battled it out wheel-to-wheel for the entire twenty-two laps. Generally Schwantz held the upper hand, with the Honda's expected top-speed advantage failing to materialise on the downhill Suzuka straight. Later it was discovered that the reed valves in the carburettor system had been incorrectly fitted, depriving the bike of about forty per cent of its top-end power. Nevertheless, Gardner clung to Schwantz like a limpet, despite some lurid slides on the exits of corners. The Australian never gave up, and schemed to pass Schwantz on the last lap at the chicane just before the finish line. But his plan came unstuck, with near-disastrous consequences. Gardner came through the right-hand sweeper before the chicane at top speed and, with Schwantz in his sights, poured on the power. However, there was too much power too soon, and the rear tyre slid sideways. Gardner had no alternative but to ride off the track at 200 kilometres per hour. Amazingly, he managed to stay upright as the bike ran across grass, gravel and then a helicopter landing pad. To huge cheers from the crowd, he rode back onto the track and still finished second—nine seconds behind Schwantz and four ahead of third-placed Eddie Lawson's Yamaha.

'I guess I was lucky to survive that one,' he said after

the race. 'If it had happened anywhere else on the track it could have been curtains for me. As it was, the fences were well back there because of the chopper pad. Lucky there wasn't a chopper on it! And I still got second place, so I can't complain.'

That evening, Lawson was an unexpected gate-crasher at the Honda party at Suzuka Circuit. The normally taciturn American surprised everyone with his warmth and conviviality that night, and 'kicked on' with Gardner and the Honda crew until well past midnight. Gardner enjoyed the night immensely, and when the pair filmed a motorcycle safety television commercial in the United States the next week, Gardner declared that the hatchet was buried between him and the man he'd deposed as world champion. He could put aside Lawson's non-appearance on the rostrum in Brazil the previous year when he'd won the world championship, and the well-publicised bitching between the two.

From Japan, the GP circus headed across the northern Pacific to California, and Laguna Seca on the Monterey Peninsula. It was the first United States Grand Prix since 1965, but facilities there were poor and the track was dangerous. Gardner disliked it immediately, and this showed in his lap times during qualifying. 'We have been a little erratic with the times and it has been hard work both mentally and physically,' he said during a break in practice, as he sought treatment for blistered hands from wrestling the Honda around the bumpy, winding circuit. His Honda didn't like it either, and the altered steering geometry, which aimed to move the weight back onto the rear wheel in order to reduce wheelspin under acceleration, clearly was not working. In the race, the bike behaved more like a bucking bronco from the Wild West than a sophisticated racing machine, threatening to throw Gardner off numerous times during the forty-lap race. To make matters worse, his front brake pads wore out completely and he rode with metal grinding on metal for the final ten laps. When he stopped the bike, the front discs were so hot that the metal welded together, and the mechanics were unable to wheel the bike away.

Nevertheless, Gardner showed the fighting spirit he is so respected for by forcing himself to ride over his problems. Lawson ran away with the race on a Yamaha that clearly handled the bumpy surface much better, while Gardner battled through for second place, overtaking Scot Niall MacKenzie with six laps to go, despite having no front brake. Gardner was deeply concerned about his machine's handling problems, but put a brave face on it by declaring things would be different when the teams got to familiar territory in Europe. And after two rounds of the championship he had scored two seconds to put him in second place, just one point behind Lawson. Things certainly weren't desperate—yet.

But the picture didn't improve in Europe. In fact, it got steadily worse as the shortcomings of the NSR500 were brutally exposed. Third at Jarama in the Spanish Grand Prix was followed by fifth at Jerez in the Portuguese Grand Prix. Gardner was still second in the championship, but in two races he'd slipped from one to twelve points behind. In desperation, Gardner asked Honda to take his 1987 bike out of mothballs. 'Honda seems to have taken one step forward and ten steps back,' he said after the Portuguese race. 'What worked so well last year is now causing problems, and other problems have emerged that just weren't happening last year. The bike is fast enough, but the handling, suspension and braking leave a lot to be desired. The bike starts sliding in the corners before I start accelerating, and the overall effect is pretty frightening. My riding style has always involved sliding and it isn't that which frightens me. But in the past I had control of my slides. Now I just don't know what to expect. The problem most definitely is the chassis, and the entire geometry of the frame seems to be right out. The weight distribution is all wrong. Eddie Lawson reckons the bike looks like it has a huge hinge in the middle, with the front and back end floating free, and that's just how it feels. I think Eddie actually feels sorry for me, even though he's enjoying giving me a thrashing.'

Honda refused to give Gardner his old bike back, reasoning that it would be a massive loss of face were they to admit that they had made a mistake—even though it was obvious to even the most casual observer. However, the factory did agree to modify the '87 frame to accommodate the '88 engine, and to make various other changes to the steering-head angle and brakes. The engine was moved back and the design engineers raised the pivot point where the swinging arm that holds the rear wheel joins the main frame. The aim was to put even more weight on the rear wheel to reduce wheelspin. There was a three-week break between the Portuguese GP and the Italian, so the Rothmans Honda team booked the Rijeka track in Yugoslavia and spent three days testing the new equipment. The changes seemed to work, and Gardner was able to lap consistently under the Rijeka lap record he had set winning the GP there the previous year. But just when Gardner thought the bike was finally friendlier towards him, it spat him off after a particularly vicious slide. The result was six broken bones in his left foot.

Gardner arrived at Imola for the Italian Grand Prix determined to grin and bear the pain of his broken foot. He kept the extent of the injury a secret, for fear officials would rule him unfit. All he would admit was that his foot was bruised and swollen. The Grand Prix medical officer, Italian doctor Claudio Costa, fashioned a special cast to fit around his damaged foot so that he would be able to change gears without doing further damage. Then, in a performance of considerable courage, the plucky Australian surprised even himself by claiming pole position—his first of the season. 'I never thought I'd get to the stage of racing with broken bones, but I was desperate,' Gardner recalls. 'I knew if I didn't get out there and go for a good result, I could kiss the championship goodbye. I wasn't about to let that happen without a damn good fight.' Team manager Jerry Burgess admits Gardner's performance to claim pole position brought a lump to his throat realising just how much effort his rider was putting in.

Imola is one of the fastest tracks in Europe, with awesomely quick sweeping corners that truly separate the men from the boys. Lawson and Gardner proved themselves the men in the Italian Grand Prix, quickly separating themselves from the pack and settling down for a two-man duel. Lawson held the upper hand, but Gardner hung on tenaciously to his back wheel for the first fifteen of the twenty-five laps. But on the sixteenth lap Gardner ran wide on a fast corner and got into a slide. 'I banged my foot on the curb trying to correct the slide, and that was it,' Gardner recalls. 'It hurt like hell and I had to back off. I thought I had a chance up to then, despite the pain of changing gears, but once I hit my foot I had to ease off and be happy with second place.' However, Gardner was so pleased to have finished at all that he donated his entire prize money, some $16,000, to Dr Costa.

It seemed an extraordinarily generous gesture, but Gardner didn't see it that way. 'It was no big deal. Dr Costa's work at each track is voluntary and without him I couldn't have ridden. Besides, I knew he was trying to establish his clinic and needed the money. He is a fantastic guy who helps the riders more than most of them realise, and I wanted to show my appreciation. Besides, the seventeen points I got for second place kept my championship hopes alive, so it was a small price to pay. Anyway, he deserved it.'

A week later the GP circus was at the Nurburgring for the West German GP, and although still discomforted by his injured foot, Gardner again claimed pole position. He did it in the best traditions of his '87 championship year, flashing across the line on the last lap of official qualifying to knock off four tenths of a second from Yamaha rider Wayne Rainey's previous best time. It seemed that the old Wayne Gardner was back, but the race proved a bitter disappointment. Riding in appalling, wet conditions, Gardner faltered from the start. When the flag dropped Gardner gunned the throttle, but the rear wheel spun viciously on the wet track and the bike went sideways. By the time he got going, most of the field had streamed past. Coming from well back is almost impossible in the rain, because of the spray coming from riders in front. With his injured foot still troubling him, Gardner struggled home in eighth position, while Schwantz swept to an easy victory on his Suzuki.

The season was approaching the halfway stage and the defending world champion had yet to record a victory. Few could believe it, least of all Gardner. He was bitterly disappointed as he headed for Austria a full twenty points behind Lawson in the title chase. Not even news from home that he'd been awarded an Order of Australia Medal in the Queen's birthday honours list could cheer him.

The daunting and dangerous Salzburgring is no place for the desperate, but Gardner was more than that as he prepared for the Austrian Grand Prix. He knew he had to win, and Phil

Leading Eddie Lawson down Laguna Seca's infamous Corkscrew during the 1988 United States Grand Prix (Franco Villani)

Racing memorabilia, including Wayne's 1987 World Championship—winning bike (re-numbered) at Wayne Gardner Enterprises' Wollongong offices (Peter Geran)

Gardner leads Christian Sarron (4), Wayne Rainey (3) and Kevin Magee (5) through Honda Corner during the Australian Grand Prix, Phillip Island, 1989 (Peter Geran)

The final lap of the first Australian Grand Prix, and Gardner leads Rainey (3), Sarron (4) and Magee. That's how they finished (Peter Geran)

The victory lap at the first Australian Grand Prix—with Wayne proudly carrying his flag as the fans sweep across the track to cheer him, Phillip Island 1989 (Peter Geran)

Back to pit lane and a big welcome from Donna and the rest of the team—Australian Grand Prix, 1989 (Leon Faivre)

The Australian fans spill out across the Phillip Island circuit to hail their hero after Gardner wins his country's first Grand Prix, Phillip Island, 1989 (Peter Geran)

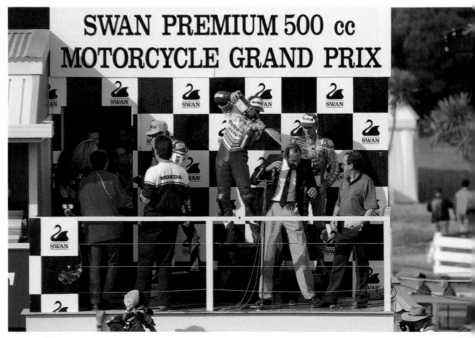

Cop that! Gardner gives promoter Bob Barnard a champagne shower on the rostrum after winning the first Australian Grand Prix (Peter Geran)

Fearon was on hand to psyche him up for the race of his life. For the first sixteen laps it was indeed that. He and Lawson battled it out wheel-to-wheel on the 300-kilometre-per-hour climb up the hill behind the pits, round the downhill speed banking, through the chicane, and down the pit straight to the bottom of the hill before the climb back up again. In motor sport there is probably no sight more awesome than two champions duelling at close quarters on the very dangerous Salzburgring, and the 80,000 spectators clustered on the Alpine hillsides were enthralled by the battle unfolding below them. First Gardner led, then Lawson, then Gardner, then Lawson again, and so on. It was absolutely rivetting, with hardly a bike's length separating the pair for the first sixteen laps and the lead changing almost every lap. Then disaster struck.

At the end of lap sixteen Gardner felt the engine tighten and he pulled in the clutch just as he was entering the long right-hander at the top of the hill. 'I couldn't believe the engine had seized so far into the race, so I thought maybe it was just the brakes dragging. I let the clutch out to see if the engine would restart but it just locked solid, and threw me off.' Gardner crash-landed on his head, but managed to walk away. 'That's the championship over for me,' he said after the race. 'Eddie's now forty points ahead and there is no way I can make that up. It is so frustrating. We finally got the Honda working properly after all our problems this year, and I felt I could win this race.'

The realisation that his dream of defending the title was over had a deep effect on Gardner. The next day he and Donna, with an Australian couple visiting them, drove from Salzburg to their home in Monaco. It felt like driving to the funeral of a much-loved relative. Gardner was mourning the grim reality that the title he had taken ten long years to win had slipped through his fingers in ten short weeks. He hammered the rented five-series BMW, and conversation during the ten-hour journey was restricted to brief outbursts surfacing painfully every half or so. In between, Gardner lapsed into deep and melancholy reflection as his mind churned over the events of the previous day. It was a journey none of the four in the car that day is ever likely to forget.

But Gardner is no quitter, as he has shown time and

time again. His championship hopes may have been over, but he still had something to ride for—pride. The next race was the Dutch Grand Prix at Assen, and Gardner went into it with his self-confidence at an all-time low. 'I was really starting to doubt my own ability,' Gardner recalls. 'I thought it was the bike that had been causing the problems, but in the end I didn't know what to think—was it me, or was it the bike? I lost all my confidence and was really starting to worry that I'd lost whatever it takes to win—that little bit extra that seems to separate the top guys from the rest of the field. It was a really bad time in my life and it started raising doubts in my mind about all sorts of things.' Gardner was also concerned that people back home in Australia would consider him a quitter, or a one-season wonder who couldn't be bothered putting in the effort required to defend his title. He needn't have worried on that score. The evidence was clear on the live telecasts of every race. Gardner didn't have a PR problem, but Honda did.

But if Gardner felt he couldn't win at Assen, that wasn't apparent to anyone at the track. He was right up with the leaders throughout qualifying, and started from fourth place on the grid. When the flag dropped, Lawson grabbed the lead, but Gardner stalked him as a wolf stalks his prey. On lap fifteen he nipped past and into the lead, then pulled steadily away to win by eleven seconds. The relief was enormous, and that night Gardner celebrated long and hard. 'It was as though a cloud of bad luck had finally been lifted off me,' he recalls. 'That win was one of the sweetest I've ever had, because I proved to myself I could still do it. That was very important to me,' he recalls. And there was more to come: Gardner won the next two GPs in Belgium and Yugoslavia to open up, ever so slightly, the world championship door that seemed to have slammed so firmly in his face.

By the time the teams headed for the Paul Ricard Circuit in the south of France for the French GP, Gardner was back to twenty points behind Lawson. In three races he had cut the forty-point deficit by half, and with six rounds to go there was still a glimmer of hope. The race was superb, one of the best in years, with Gardner, Lawson, Schwantz and local hero Christian Sarron drawing away and engaging in a four-way battle. The dicing was unforgettable, with all four riders taking turns at the lead amid some breathtaking slip-streaming down the 310-kilometre-per-hour Mistral Straight. But through it all Gardner kept a cool head, sizing up his opponents and working on a strategy that would give him victory. With five laps to go Gardner started pushing himself and his machine just a little harder, and edged away from the others. Going into the last lap he had a three-second cushion, and victory seemed assured.

But as the saying goes, nothing is certain until the flag drops. Going down the Mistral Straight for the last time Gardner felt his engine tighten. The head of a bolt in the engine had sheered off and been sucked into the water pump. It chewed the pump to pieces, and the coolant gushed into the oil pump and gearbox, flushing the oil out over Gardner's leg. Deprived of coolant and oil, the engine inevitably seized. Gardner coasted the remaining few hundred metres to the chequered flag, but Lawson, Sarron and Schwantz had all passed him by the time he got there. A big fist-sized indentation in the top of Gardner's fuel tank was evidence enough of his bitterness and frustration at yet another machine failure. After the race he let Honda have the full force of his fury.

'That's twice Honda have let me down badly. It seems they are just handing the title to Yamaha,' he said. 'That race was the biggest disappointment of my career. I went out there to win the race and pull some more points back on Eddie, so I could really put some pressure on him in the last five races of the season. I also wanted to prove I am the fastest rider in the world. I think I did that out on the track, but I don't have the points to prove it. That was a real dogfight out there. No-one gave an inch and we all touched fairings a couple of times. It was heavy stuff and I put everything into it. I timed my run to go for a break with three laps to go, and going into the last lap I was three seconds up. To have that ruined by machine failure on the last lap is just so heartbreaking.'

As things turned out, Gardner had every right to be bitter about his machine. He wound up his season with second placings in Britain, Sweden and Brazil and a win in Czechoslovakia to finish more strongly than Lawson, and only twenty-three points behind. In Czechoslovakia Gardner shattered the lap record by more than two and a half seconds in qualifying, then romped away with the race in one of the most commanding performances of the season. But it was all to no avail: before the race he and the other riders had voted to boycott the Argentinean GP because promised circuit safety improvements had not been carried out. Gardner led the riders' revolt, even though it destroyed his faint hopes of winning the championship. 'Personally I don't want to race in Argentina. The track is dangerous and last year we were treated like idiots,' he said at the time, adding that he was disappointed that Lawson didn't take a similarly strong stand on the safety issue. Lawson retorted: 'I wasn't going to go [to the riders' meeting] and have him [Gardner] flap his lip about how he is giving me the world championship. I want to go to Argentina because I want to beat him on all circuits.' Old wounds between the two were reopened.

Despite the early-season problems with handling, ultimately it was the machine failures in Austria and France which cost Gardner the world title. If he had won in Austria and France, he would have finished with twenty-seven more points. Lawson, on the other hand, would have finished with six less than he ultimately achieved by being relegated to second in each race. Gardner could have had 256 points to Lawson's 248, instead of the American winning with 252 to Gardner's 229.

Of course there are plenty of 'if only' situations in any sport. The only points that count are the ones on the board and Lawson had them where it counted. Nevertheless, motorcycle racing's most authoritative journal, Peter Clifford's *Motocourse Annual*, had no hesitation in naming Gardner the number-one rider in its top ten from all classes for 1988. Clifford wrote: 'In 1988 it [the Honda] was obviously not in the same class as the Yamahas but that never stopped Gardner riding it way beyond the limit of its possibilities. He pushed the NSR harder than anyone else could have done—and that makes him the best rider in the world. Gardner's incredible ability to ride a machine hard, to keep it going on any circuit and to maintain that approach for the entire season makes him the best rider.' Clifford continued: 'With luck he will be given a competitive machine for 1989 and will continue to speak his mind, carry on letting his hair down with the old friends who have always appreciated him, and ride in the dramatic, all-action style that pushes the envelope with every front or rear wheel slide, dragging knee, glowing disc and lap record.'

The year took its toll on Gardner's personal life as well. He and Donna had planned to marry in November 1988, but as the pressure mounted Gardner felt more and more alienated by his on-track problems, and he took out his frustrations on those closest to him. Eventually, he decided he couldn't go through with his wedding, and called it off. At the time, the official reason was that he would have to spend November overseas testing to make sure he and Honda were fully prepared for the 1989 season. That was one part of the story.

The other side of the story wasn't publicly revealed until Wayne and Donna did an interview with an Australian television magazine in March 1989. Then Gardner frankly admitted that he had got cold feet—that the pressures and disappointments of the season had been too great, and he had been unable to contemplate a wedding as well. Not surprisingly, Donna was disappointed. 'What woman wouldn't be?' she says. 'We had planned to invite so many people who had helped Wayne along the way over the years. It would have been a great way to thank them all, as well as a reunion for all our family and friends. However, I understood what was happening to Wayne and I didn't want to put any more pressure on him.' Donna reasoned that since she had waited ten years another year wouldn't matter. The couple set a new wedding date: 18 November 1989.

Despite the disappointments of 1988, Gardner considered he could look back on the season with some satisfaction. He had salvaged second place in the championship out of the wreckage, and felt he had learned valuable lessons that would set the team and factory up for 1989. 'With all the problems we had, and having to solve them as the season continued, I gained so much understanding about what is needed in terms of suspension and frames. I told Honda we'd have to start development for the next season as soon as the last Grand Prix was over—and that's what we did, staying on in Brazil for testing after we'd raced there. I was already planning what we'd need and how we'd do it,' he says.

So was Honda. In fact, it had been secretly planning since midway through the season. And its plans were going to give Gardner the biggest shock of his life.

CHAPTER 16

So Much for Loyalty

Y ou could argue that Wayne Gardner probably learned as much about international motor sport on 17 October 1988 as he had in all of the previous ten years. And he learned it from a news item in a London newspaper, not on the racetrack. The article said that the Rothmans Honda team had signed world champion Eddie Lawson for the 1989 season. It was the biggest sensation in Grand Prix motorcycle racing in years, and it hit Gardner like a bombshell. It taught the Australian a lesson he is never likely to forget— that loyalty does not exist in a big-money sport like this. As the story unfolded over the next few weeks, it transpired that Lawson and Honda had been secretly negotiating since the middle of the year. While Gardner had been battling machine problems and broken bones to keep Honda's flag flying proudly, the company was planning the coup of the decade—signing Gardner's arch rival, Eddie Lawson, from Marlboro Yamaha.

As a business proposition it made excellent sense. Honda would have the world's top two riders, and as a bonus Yamaha would be considerably weakened by the loss of its star. But as far as the human side was concerned, the deal stank. Honda and Lawson had been secretly plotting the switch since the Belgian GP on 3 July. Neither Honda nor Rothmans had breathed a word of it to their number-one rider, Gardner, for more than three months. Then he learned about it in the worst possible way—by reading it in a newspaper. It was a humiliating experience, and one Gardner will never forget, or forgive.

'So much for loyalty,' he said to the media at the time. 'I have been riding my butt off for Honda all year on a pig of a bike while they have been working on this for months. They didn't even have the courtesy to tell me before I read it in the papers. It is very disappointing. Honda knew exactly where I was. It couldn't possibly have been a problem for them to pick up the phone and let me know. So that's their idea of how to treat a loyal rider—it has certainly made me fully aware of how the factory acts, and what they think of their riders. It is a lesson I'll remember when my contract expires at the end of the season. If I sign up again it won't be out of loyalty, which has been a major factor in the past.'

And the bitterness hasn't disappeared since then. If anything, it is stronger after the events of the 1989 season. 'It is hard for me to forgive them,' Gardner says. 'I was out doing promotional work for Rothmans in Greece and Cyprus when the season ended while everyone was scheming behind my back. I was very bitter about it then, and it hasn't changed. They made it very difficult for me mentally, because I had to prove myself all over again. I couldn't just concentrate on giving my best for Honda to beat the other factories—I had to compete with another Honda rider who just happened to be my biggest rival. On the one hand I can accept Honda's reasons for doing it—they wanted to have the best team and you can't blame them for that—but I will never accept the way they went about it.'

The day after the Lawson signing was leaked to the English press, Gardner and his manager Harris Barnett flew to Tokyo for top-level talks with the Honda hierarchy. Gardner was in the middle of a two-year contract with Honda, and was concerned that he would be in a vulnerable position against the new signing. He and Barnett demanded equal treatment, and were given assurances that he would retain his number-one status with the factory and be given the same level of machinery and support as Lawson. Honda announced Gardner and rookie Australian Michael Doohan would comprise the official Rothmans Honda works team, while Lawson would operate in a 'satellite' team using the same machines and in the same Rothmans colours. In other words, there would be two number ones, and may the best man win. Gardner accepted that, and rejected overtures from rival teams, including Marlboro Yamaha, to break his contract.

He could even see some positive aspects to the new arrangement. Lawson would be bringing with him a vast knowledge of the Yamaha operation and machinery, and so presumably could translate that into improvements on the Honda.

129

And it would give both riders the chance to settle, once and for all, who was better. A sceptical international motorcycle media, however, predicted that friction between the two long-time rivals would erupt before the 1989 season was very old. To their credit, when the dust had settled from the shock announcement, both Lawson and Gardner took a professional approach to their new partnership. They papered over past differences, and even appeared together in a worldwide satellite media conference to profess their undying respect for each other. Gardner rather cheekily claimed that previous reports of clashes between the two were just media beat-ups, and that they were really the best of friends. Privately, he conceded that trouble lay ahead.

'Eddie and I do respect each other as riders, and when we're not racing there have been times when we have got on really well. But when the racing starts that all changes, and it won't be any different with Eddie on a Honda. If anything, it will be even more intense. You just can't put two champions in one team and expect harmony. We're too competitive for that. Honda tried it in Formula One car racing with Alain Prost and Ayrton Senna in the McLaren team, and it didn't take long for that to fall apart.'

Indeed, the McLaren experience in 1988 when the two drivers swept all before them in Formula One racing, may well have inspired Honda's decision to pair Gardner and Lawson together. However, the situation in motorcycle racing is very different from Formula One, where Honda machinery reigns supreme. Yamaha and Suzuki are more than capable of producing bikes to match Honda's, so having the number-one and number-two plates on their bikes was no guarantee of success. And if those riders didn't win, it could reflect very poorly indeed on the company's products.

So the pressure was right on Honda and its riders when the 1989 season got underway with the Japanese Grand Prix at the end of March. The fact that Honda owned the track but had not won a 500-cc world championship event there just added to the burden. Honda's approach was interesting. It called Gardner, Lawson and Doohan to a secret meeting and offered each one a bonus if he could win—US$100,000 to be exact. As if each rider did not have enough to think about, they now had a very juicy carrot dangling in front of them. It could only be a distraction.

Gardner was yet to be convinced that he was getting the same treatment as Lawson. The American had been given faster engines for pre-season testing in Brazil, although when the testing moved to Phillip Island in Australia the pair recorded virtually identical times. However, during qualifying at Suzuka, Gardner's fears touched on paranoia. Phil Fearon was on hand to help Gardner concentrate on his own performance and ignore everyone else, but it was a difficult assignment when Gardner's bike was clearly down on power. His bike was only thirteenth fastest through the radar speed trap on the main straight, a full ten kilometres per hour down on Lawson's bike. Shrugging that aside, Gardner rode like a demon to make up the difference, and qualified fourth on the grid ahead of Lawson, who was troubled by a cracked bone in his wrist—the result of a practice fall a few weeks earlier. But throughout qualifying neither of the Honda riders could match the flying Yamahas of pole-sitter Tadahiko Taira and Wayne Rainey, and Suzuki's Kevin Schwantz. $100,000 or no $100,000, the Yamahas and Suzuki were simply too fast.

And so it proved in the GP, with Rainey and Schwantz making the race their own by streaking away from the field and engaging in a spectacular man-on-man dice that saw the Suzuki star win by a whisker. Third place was the best anyone else could hope for, and Gardner was desperate to finish on the rostrum—and to beat Lawson. Perhaps he was too desperate, because by his own admission he rode one of the worst races of his career. After muffing the start and getting away seventh, Gardner ran off the track on lap two and dropped back to sixteenth. He then clawed his way through the field to pass Lawson and claim third, but ran off again on lap seventeen. This time it was more dramatic. His legs were flung in the air and he came down heavily on the tank, smashing his groin in the process. Somehow he managed to regain control without hitting the armco barrier and got back on the track as Lawson flashed past to move into third place. This time Gardner was in no condition to give chase, and had to settle for a disappointing fourth. Lawson had a great view of Gardner's near-disaster and said, 'I was right behind Wayne and saw it all. It was a real good save. I was impressed.' Gardner was not. 'I rode like a right plonker', he said after he had gingerly dismounted. 'That has to be one of the worst rides of my life.'

That night Gardner became even more painfully aware of how poorly he had ridden. His groin injury was causing considerable concern, and Gardner was in excruciating agony from the bruising and swelling. The Grand Prix medical officer, Dr Claudio Costa, was so worried that he took Gardner to hospital for X-rays. If the swelling didn't go down overnight, Costa held genuine fears that he may have to remove the left testicle. Fortunately, that wasn't necessary, but after Costa left the next morning, Gardner began to ponder how to tackle the next GP— a race he prized above all others. He was going home to Australia for his country's first-ever world championship Grand Prix, and he just had to win it.

CHAPTER 17

Australian Grand Prix Diary

Winning the inaugural Australian Grand Prix at Phillip Island in 1989 was the greatest moment in Wayne Gardner's career—a victory sweeter even than when he clinched the 1987 world championship in Brazil. But it was achieved at an enormous physical and emotional cost that left him completely drained, and a week later he was lying in an American hospital bed with his leg broken in two places after an uncharacteristic mistake led to a crash in the United States Grand Prix. It was an expensive price to pay for his ultimate triumph.

Wayne Gardner has probably never worked harder than in the week leading up to the inaugural Swan Premium Australian Grand Prix at Phillip Island on 9 April 1989. He turned himself into a one-man promotional band, giving the event enormous publicity. The reasons were twofold. Gardner was desperate for the event to succeed, and considered he could play a major role in publicising it if he went on as many television programmes as possible in the week leading up to the event. The other side of the coin was that there were plenty of television producers who wanted to highlight the race, but there really was only one man they wanted to talk to—Australia's number one. Channel Nine commentator, twice 500-cc world champion Barry Sheene, was one with deep misgivings about the amount of time Gardner was devoting to promotional duties. Despite his considerable success, Sheene had never won his home Grand Prix in Britain, weighed down as he was each year by a combination of media pressure and public expectation. The result, Sheene said, was that something always went wrong, and he was concerned the same would happen to Gardner. 'I can see why Wayne is doing it, and I think that is great, but he's mad to agree to do so much. At the end of the weekend none of the sponsors will remember who did all the promotional stuff, they'll only remember who won. They'll come and ask you why you didn't win and they won't care a hoot when you tell them you went on this TV show or that one to give them publicity. Winning the race is all they really care about,' Sheene said before the race. 'There is a big risk Wayne will burn himself out this week.'

Indeed, Gardner did admit to journalists at a press conference after the first day of official qualifying that he felt completely burnt out. And not surprisingly! His schedule over the previous week had been extremely punishing.

Gardner had flown in to Sydney from the Japanese Grand Prix on Tuesday 28 March with painfully damaged testicles after his mishap in the Suzuka race, and, despite the severe discomfort, spent the next day filming around Wollongong with the top-rating 'Burke's Backyard' television programme. Thursday and Friday were devoted to filming promotional spots with Nine's Wide World of Sports, then on Saturday he spent the day at the programme's Sydney studio, co-hosting the entire show, which runs for four hours on Saturday afternoons. On the following Monday, Gardner conducted three separate interviews with television news crews, as well as taking numerous phone calls from radio stations.

And that was just a taste of things to come. The rest of the week went like this:
WEDNESDAY 5 APRIL, 6.45 a.m.: Wayne leaves Wollongong with fiancée Donna Forbes and manager Harris Barnett to catch the 8.15 a.m. Australian Airlines flight from Sydney to Melbourne. 9.30 a.m.: Meets with Honda Australia executives on arrival at Melbourne airport to discuss promotional plans for the week. 11.00 a.m.: Checks in to Southern Cross Hotel, then heads across town to appear live on Channel Seven's Bert Newton lunchtime variety show. While he's there, Seven's news department spots him on the show and sends a crew to his dressing room for an interview. 1.05 p.m.: Drives across Melbourne to Nine's studios to record a segment of the hugely popular 'Hey, Hey It's Saturday Night', with Darryl Somers. 4.00 p.m.: Back to hotel for a shower and a brief break. 5.30 p.m.: Car collects Gardner from the Southern Cross to take him to a Lord Mayoral reception for the Grand Prix at Melbourne Town Hall, depositing him back at the hotel

an hour later. 7.30 p.m.: Gardner, Donna and Barnett go to the Grand Prix ball at the Southern Cross ballroom. A media contingent waylays them in the foyer, and they spend half an hour conducting interviews before they go in. At the ball, Gardner's 'official' duties include bringing singer Jackie Love on stage on the back of a motorcycle. But the ball is one of the more pleasant engagements for the week, and Wayne and Donna stay until midnight.

THURSDAY 6 APRIL, 7.00 a.m.: A light breakfast, and then on the road for Phillip Island, a two-hour drive from Melbourne. Honda Australia has supplied Gardner with a Legend coupé for the week, so the drive is most enjoyable. They arrive at the circuit just before 10.00 a.m., and Gardner goes straight to his team's pit garage to see his crew and discuss the bike's preparation for that afternoon's practice session. 12.00 a.m.: A light lunch of cold meat and salad, and Gardner climbs into his leather racing suit and by 1.15 p.m. is ready for action. 1.25 p.m.: He and fellow Australian 500-cc riders Kevin Magee and Michael Doohan are given a lap of honour together to 'christen' the track before the hour-long free practice session starts. This session means little. It is a shakedown run for the riders and their machines, so that they are well set up and familiar with the circuit by the time official qualifying starts the next day. Nevertheless, all the teams keep a watchful eye on each other's lap times, and Gardner is reasonably happy to be fourth fastest. At least the lack of top speed that troubled him in Japan has been largely remedied by a new engine that has arrived the day before from Honda Racing headquarters in Tokyo. He uses both his bikes, so that he can evaluate different suspension settings, tyres and gearing. 2.30 p.m.: Free practice finishes, and Gardner goes straight into a debriefing with team manager Stuart Shenton (who replaced Jerry Burgess in 1989) and HRC technicians to discuss how the bikes should be set up for the next day. 4.00 p.m.: Goes straight to a press conference with the other Rothmans Honda riders, Michael Doohan and Eddie Lawson. 5.00 p.m.: The press conference is over, and Gardner escapes with Donna back to the hotel at Cowes, on the other side of Phillip Island. He is exhausted, and orders a steak dinner from room service, before slumping in front of the television. 9.30 p.m.: Gardner is in bed.

FRIDAY 7 APRIL, 7.00 a.m.: Gardner leaves for the circuit, where he is scheduled to appear on a live cross to Channel Nine's breakfast programme, 'The Today Show', at 7.35. Amazingly, the security guard at the gate to Nine's compound won't let Gardner in because he doesn't have the right pass. He is about to leave in disgust, when an embarrassed television producer rushes out and ushers him through. 8.00 a.m.: Gardner is scheduled to appear on a radio programme with Melbourne's 3MMM-FM. Once again, a security guard refuses him access to the on-track radio studio. By now thoroughly annoyed, Gardner escapes to the Rothmans hospitality unit for an early breakfast of fresh fruit, croissants and coffee. Race promoter Bob Barnard drops in for a chat over coffee. 8.40 a.m.: 3MMM staff track Gardner down and apologise profusely for the overly officious security guard, and this time escort him through to their studio. 9.00 a.m.: His radio duties completed, Gardner walks straight into an interview with Nine Sport's Darryl Eastlake, before fleeing to the sanctity of the pit garage, where he can get down to work with the team. 10.40 a.m.: The first of four forty-minute qualifying sessions. Gardner is experimenting with suspension settings, but is still not altogether pleased to be shunted down to fifth fastest. After a pit-lane interview with Nine's Barry Sheene, he spends an hour with Shenton and the HRC men plotting machine strategies for the afternoon session. 12.20 p.m.: Gardner spends fifteen minutes with a severely disabled boy suffering from muscular dystrophy. The Make a Wish Foundation has requested that Gardner meet the boy, and he is only too happy to oblige, showering the boy with gifts from Honda, including a remote-controlled motorcycle and Grand Prix clothing. A Channel Ten news crew spots Gardner and grabs him for a quick interview. 12.45 p.m.: Peace at last, as Gardner escapes to the Rothmans suite for lunch. Once again he eats sparingly—a little cold meat and salad. 1.50 p.m.: Back out on the circuit for the second qualifying session. This time everything works perfectly, and Gardner puts in a succession of extremely quick laps to dominate the session. However, Yamaha ace Wayne Rainey comes up with a super-fast lap minutes from the end of the session, to just pip Gardner's time. Nevertheless, the Australian is satisfied with the afternoon's work, and becomes more confident that he can give Sunday's race a shake. He is happy to do another pit-lane interview with Sheene. In the meantime, Harris Barnett has phoned Honda Australia's PR chief and cancelled a planned promotional appearance in Melbourne that night. Honda wanted to send a helicopter to Phillip Island to collect Gardner and take him to Melbourne for a dinner dance for Honda dealers. Barnett has put his foot down: 'Sorry, but such a trip in the middle of qualifying would seriously jeopardise Gardner's chances of winning the race.' 2.30 p.m.: The afternoon debriefing with Shenton lasts one and a half hours as further machine changes are mulled over for Saturday's qualifying. 4.15 p.m.: Gardner attends the usual Rothmans press conference at the media centre. This time most of the interest surrounds Lawson and Doohan, who both crashed in the afternoon session. 4.45 p.m.: Gardner conducts a separate media conference with film-makers, who announce a five-million-dollar mini-series based on his life story. 5.00 p.m.: An English film crew grabs Gardner for an interview as he leaves the media centre. Is there no end? 5.30 p.m.: Back to the hotel to relax. Wayne and Donna and a few friends watch the 'Burke's Backyard' programme he features in, then go out for dinner in Cowes at 8.30. He's in bed by 10. Sure beats a night chopper ride to Melbourne.

SATURDAY 8 APRIL, 7.30 a.m.: Breakfast of bacon and eggs at the hotel, then out to the track at 8.00 a.m. to link up with the team. They have decided to experiment with different steering geometry to make the bike steer faster so that Gardner can take a tighter line through the slower corners. 10.40 a.m.: Qualifying starts, but the changes haven't worked, and Gardner can't get close to the times he was doing the previous day. To make matters worse, a pathetically slow German rider called Michel Rudroff falls down at the hairpin corner and takes Gardner with him, wrecking his NSR500. Gardner runs back to the pits to get on his spare bike, but it is too slow and after a few laps he parks it and fumes at his forced inaction as the other riders complete the last twenty minutes of the session. Sheene grabs Gardner for a quick interview in pit lane. The mechanics start work repairing the wrecked bike. 1.50 p.m.: After the debriefing and a light lunch, Gardner is back out on the track again, trying once again to make the steering changes work. They don't, and Friday's best lap time of 1:35.77 still stands for Gardner. However, Texan Suzuki ace Kevin Schwantz has taken over the front-running from Rainey, and grabs pole position with a blistering time of 1:34.99. Gardner is relegated to third on the grid. He doesn't mind that, because anywhere on the front row is good enough, but he is very concerned at the outright speed advantage of Schwantz's Suzuki. During yet another interview he tells Sheene that Schwantz will be very hard to beat. At the afternoon debriefing with Shenton, they decide to revert back to Friday's settings and simply ride around the problem of slow steering. At least the bike is stable in the corners and quick down the straight, although not as quick as the Suzuki. 4.15 p.m.: Another three-way press conference with the other Rothmans Honda riders, then Gardner has more interviews with English and Italian television crews. 5.30 p.m.: Gardner leaves the circuit to be confronted by a monumental traffic jam. Never one to sit patiently, he spots an ambulance heading down the wrong side of the road with lights flashing, nips in behind, and gets a ride in its slipstream all the way through to Cowes. A police officer finally halts him, but lets him through when he discovers who is driving. 6.30 p.m.: Wayne and Donna order room service again, and spend the evening watching television. 8.45 p.m.: Wayne slips away for a massage from the team's physiotherapist to iron out a few slight bruises and pains from that morning's practice fall. 10.00 p.m. In bed and sleeping soundly. (Pre-race nerves rarely prevent Gardner getting a good night's sleep.)

SUNDAY 9 APRIL, 7.30 a.m.: Breakfast of two boiled eggs at the hotel dining-room. 8.30 a.m.: Off to the circuit. While the spectators queue for hours to get to the public carparks, Gardner is allowed through some closed-off access roads and arrives at the track in thirty minutes. He drops in to see the team, then escapes to a hired motorhome to watch the 125-cc and 250-cc warm-up sessions on television. Shenton joins him to discuss tyre choice for the race, because it is cooler than for the previous two days of qualifying. They elect to run a slightly softer compound than they had originally planned, and decide to scrub the tyres in for a few laps during the morning's fifteen-minute warm-up. 10.10 a.m.: Gardner dons his leathers and protective gear in front of a Channel Nine video camera for some 'colour' footage for that

Taking time out to meet a young fan in a wheelchair—1989 Australian Grand Prix, Phillip Island (Leon Faivre)

Being a spectator at the 1989 Yugoslav Grand Prix after breaking his leg two months earlier (Patrick Gosling)

Australia's three Grand Prix stars, from left Michael Doohan, Wayne Gardner and Kevin Magee being interviewed for Australian television— Dutch Grand Prix, 1989 (Malcolm Bryan/Rothmans Press Service)

The comeback ride from his broken leg—Gardner gets last minute encouragement from mechanic and friend Wilf Needham, Dutch Grand Prix, 1989 (Malcolm Bryan/Rothmans Press Service)

Donna, team manager Stuart Shenton (centre) and the mechanics wait anxiously for their man during Gardner's comeback ride at the 1989 Dutch Grand Prix (Malcolm Bryan/Rothmans Press Service)

Frozen in time—coming through the Assen chicane during the 1989 Dutch Grand Prix (Patrick Gosling)

'Back on the gas' at Le Mans in the 1989 French Grand Prix (Malcolm Bryan/Rothmans Press Service)

The Spirit of Competition—one man and his motorcycle—1989 French Grand Prix at Le Mans (Malcolm Bryan/Rothmans Press Service)

afternoon's race telecast. 10.40 a.m.: The warm-up starts, but Gardner completes only a few laps, pulling in when he is satisfied that his tyres are scrubbed in and ready for the race. There is general consternation around the spectator areas, with fears Gardner has been knocked off his bike again by a slow rider. He is happy with the bike and the tyres, but desperately concerned about Schwantz. He feels he has every other rider's measure, but can't see a way to combat the Suzuki's speed advantage combined with Schwantz's confident and aggressive riding. 11.30 a.m.: Gardner wants to have lunch, but one look at the crowded Rothmans suite convinces him otherwise. He escapes to the motorhome with a bowl of pasta, staying there to watch the 250-cc Grand Prix at 12.50 p.m.. Spanish Honda star Sito Pons wins the GP, just pipping Yamaha's Jean-Phillippe Ruggia by half a bike length in a desperate run for the line. (Gardner likes to spend a lot of time alone before a race, watching television and contemplating the job ahead. Sometimes he is detached and almost trance-like as his total attention is focused on the race. Donna knows it is important to leave him alone at this time, and makes sure others do too. But today he is lucid and friendly, belying the pressure he feels as the only realistic hope Australia has of winning the country's first world championship Grand Prix.) 1.30 p.m.: Gardner dresses for business—slowly, deliberately, checking that everything is in place—back, arm, knee and shin protectors—even a groin protector, after his painful experience in Japan. The Kushitani leather suit weighs eight kilos and Gardner is convinced it is the best protection in the world. Donna completes the pre-race ritual of drawing a tiny horseshoe on his leathers. It's a good luck charm that harks back to his earliest days of racing, when his mother started the practice. 1.55 p.m.: He joins the team in pit lane and completely ignores a microphone thrust in his face by an over-enthusiastic track commentator. The time for talk is long gone. A mighty roar goes up around the circuit as he and the other riders complete their warm-up lap. The tension is electric as the riders return to the start line and take up their grid positions. Pit straight is a seething mass of people—photographers, mechanics, sponsors' girls, officials, well-wishers. Gardner speaks briefly with Shenton, advising him that all felt well with the bike on the warm-up, then stares fixedly ahead, blocking out everything but the job in hand. 2.14 p.m.: The grid is finally clear of all but the gladiators on their 170-horsepower steeds. 2.15 p.m.: The light turns green and they're off, with a deafening roar and a cloud of blue smoke. Rainey streaks to an early lead, followed by Schwantz, Tadahiko Taira and Gardner. Less than a lap completed, and Schwantz is flicked off his bike after he accelerates too hard out of a slow corner on cold tyres. (Gardner later admitted he 'got excited' at that point. 'When I saw Kevin crash I thought I might have a good chance of winning,' Gardner was to tell a post-race press conference.) Right now though, Rainey is the problem—still out in front and looking good, while his Lucky Strike Yamaha team-mate Kevin Magee has taken advantage of Schwantz's fall to slip in front of Gardner. On lap three of the thirty, Gardner passes Magee and Taira within 100 metres, and sets out after Rainey, reeling him in relentlessly lap after lap. On lap nine he is with the leader, and in front the next time around. However, Rainey is not finished, and for the next twenty laps the lead switches an incredible nineteen times as the pair, now joined by Frenchman Christian Sarron, battle it out on Phillip Island's ultra-fast bends. Gardner's periods in the lead are marked by wildly enthusiastic cheering from the vast crowd as they will their hero to victory. Finally, with three laps to go, Gardner takes charge of the race and shuts the door on his pursuers at every corner. There is no way past. 3.03 p.m.: Gardner takes the chequered flag from Rainey, Sarron and Magee—with just two seconds separating the first four placegetters. There's hardly a dry eye amongst 92,000 spectators as the Grand Prix fairytale comes to a perfect ending. The partisan crowd goes wild with delight, spilling onto the circuit to celebrate the magic of the moment as Gardner rides slowly through the throng—Australian flag held proudly aloft. He is crying inside his helmet, overwhelmed with emotion and relieved that the spectators can't see his tears. As he returns to the pit straight, Donna cannot hold back any longer, and runs up the track to throw her arms around her man. His team joins them and everyone is crying— with a mixture of delight and relief. By now Gardner doesn't care who sees his tears. Soon bike and rider are engulfed in a throng of people as thousands of spectators spill out across the track. 3.30 p.m.: Up on the rostrum in front of a sea of faces, Gardner thanks the crowd for their fantastic support and tells them he won it for them, and that it is the greatest moment of his life. More wild cheering. Someone in the crowd yells an inquiry about his 'family jewels'—a reference to the groin injury suffered at Suzuka. 'I rode my balls off in this race,' Gardner replies spontaneously, to wild acclaim. A journalist watching the proceedings comments: 'You can take the boy out of Wollongong, but you can't take Wollongong out of the boy', but that is the magic of the man. Success, fame and fortune haven't changed him. He's still a down-to-earth Aussie and the crowd loves him for it. An emotional presentation ceremony completed, champagne duly sprayed on all and sundry, Gardner, Rainey and Sarron face the customary post-race press conference, before an English television crew moves in. Then it's across to the Channel Nine on-track studio for a live interview. 5.05 p.m.: Gardner finally escapes the clutches of the media and gets back to the Rothmans suite, where his family and friends have joined the Rothmans guests to celebrate the victory. Moet and Chandon champagne and Swan Premium Lager are flowing freely. 7.45 p.m.: Swan executives arrive and whisk Gardner away to a race sponsors' party for 1000 guests, where he receives a huge reception. He gets a big laugh when he starts his speech by saying, 'Who said I'd never make it!', a reference to the theme of his first Swan Lager commercial. 8.10 p.m.: The official duties of the day finally over, Gardner returns to the Rothmans suite to farewell his family. He is leaving for the United States early the next morning and won't see them for six months. 9.35 p.m.: Wayne and Donna slip quietly away to the hotel in Cowes, but at 10.00 p.m. Gardner has to meet several journalists for one last interview. The interview turns into a celebration drinking session with some of his team, and Gardner finally finds his way to bed at 2.00 a.m. It's been quite a day.

CHAPTER 18

A Shattering Experience

W ayne Garder went from hero to zero in one week. Or at least that's how he viewed the calamitous crash in the United States Grand Prix at Laguna Seca. That it came just one week after the euphoria of the Australian Grand Prix victory seemed to rub salt into his considerable wounds. The crash left Gardner with a shattered left leg—broken just below the knee and just above the ankle. It certainly shattered his hopes of winning the world championship again in 1989, and ended his showdown with Eddie Lawson almost before it had begun. Harris Barnett estimates the crash cost Gardner more than half a million dollars in lost prizemoney and bonuses, although Honda showed him a new brand of loyalty by not exercising contractual options to reduce his retainer proportional to the races he missed. It was also Gardner's first crash in a Grand Prix in seven years that he considered his fault, and that hurt almost as much as the pain in his leg and his hip-pocket. But there was much more to the crash than Gardner making a simple, and uncharacteristic, mistake.

Gardner arrived in California physically and emotionally drained after the events at Phillip Island. His great dream of winning his home GP had come true, but here he was a few days later half-way around the world having to build himself up again for another race that was equally important—in world championship terms at least—as the Australian Grand Prix. The bike wasn't sorted out to his liking, especially for the bumpy and dangerous Laguna Seca track that he hated. To make matters worse all the bikes and equipment being air-freighted from Australia were delayed through customs, and the practice sessions had to be reduced from five to three. The team was trying to sort out a new carbon-fibre front disc brake, but things weren't going well and Gardner went down three times in practice— once at high speed when the front wheel locked up going down the straight. And then there was the Eddie Lawson factor. Gardner felt a deep personal need to beat his new Rothmans Honda team-mate on his home turf.

Despite the three falls in practice, Gardner was still third on the grid for the US GP, just behind Rainey and Schwantz and, most importantly, more than half a second ahead of Lawson who was the sixth fastest. When the flag dropped Rainey and Schwantz jumped to an early lead while Lawson was third, holding off Gardner and Kevin Magee. On lap four Gardner nipped inside Lawson on the final turn into the main straight, but Magee managed to get past both of them. Gardner chased his fellow-Australian for the next seven laps, getting more and more frustrated as he could see Rainey and Schwantz disappearing into the distance. Finally, frustration got the better of him, and he passed Magee on the first of two left-hand bends. He got past, but didn't allow himself enough room to get back on line for the next left-hander. As his bike slid across the track he could see a wall looming. Desperate not to hit it, he put his left leg out to try to steady the machine. His boot caught on the kerbing and twisted the leg violently, shattering the tibia in two places. 'Apparently, the leg can twist 10 or 20 degrees without breaking,' says Gardner, who now knows a lot more about anatomy than he did when he had his first race crash and broke his collarbone at Oran Park back in 1977. 'This must have gone a fair bit further and it exploded—just like if you were to twist a bread stick. It's apparently called a spiral fracture because the breaks spiral upward. The leg was broken before I fell off. I didn't do any further damage when I hit the dirt, but when I tried to stand up I just felt my leg go crunch and I thought: "Oh no, I've done something bad this time". It was strange, because I'd got to a point where I was riding and thinking I couldn't get hurt—like I was invincible or something. I'd gone all those years without a serious injury and somehow I didn't think it could happen to me. But it sure did this time.

'The accident was my fault. I got into the corner too hot, tried to turn the front wheel and couldn't. I lost it, picked it up, then lost it again. I banged my foot hard on the kerbing and that's where I broke it, but there was no run-off on that corner. If I had tried to ride it out I would have gone straight into a barrier. I had to lay it down.' While Gardner blames himself for the physical act of losing control of his motorcycle, and the consequences, it is not the whole story. There is little doubt he was burnt out from the demands of building himself up for Phillip Island, and the almost super-human effort to win the Australian Grand Prix. But more than that, having Lawson on the team was also a factor. Later in the season, Gardner was to tell senior Honda executives he felt they had to carry some responsibility for his crash because of the pressure they had placed him under by signing Lawson. He told them Lawson signing with Honda was one of the reasons he had a broken leg, that they had placed him in a position where he felt he had to prove he was better than Eddie every time he went out to ride. 'The result was that I was riding over the top at Laguna Seca, made a mistake and crashed and broke my leg. It was my fault, but they had to carry some of the responsibility.'

After the crash, Gardner was carted off to Monterey Community Hospital as Rainey won the GP easing down from Schwantz, while Lawson came through for third when Magee ran low on fuel late in the race. As Gardner was being wheeled into the x-ray room he was handed a telephone—the first of scores of media inquiries that were to plague him over the next few days as he battled physical pain and the acute disappointment of realising his season was as good as over. Indeed, the American doctors at the hospital said the fractures were so bad that Gardner would be out of action for at least six months. However, his friend, GP medical officer Dr Claudio Costa, had different ideas. He said if Gardner wanted the fractures pinned he could have him back on the track in a month. If he wanted to allow the leg to heal naturally, Costa could have him racing again in nine or 10 weeks.

Gardner took the second option. 'I always promised myself I wouldn't race with pins and plates and screws holding me together,' he says. 'I want to get out of racing in one piece, not all misshapen or with one leg shorter than the other or whatever. Besides, there wasn't much point rushing back. The championship went out the window for me when I crashed, so there wasn't much to be gained by rushing back.' He elected to try for a return to racing at the Dutch Grand Prix on June 24, which meant he would miss the Spanish, Italian, West German, Austrian and Yugoslav GPs. Gardner came under some pressure to change his mind and return to racing earlier than planned, and admits he almost broke his resolve on several occasions. But, in the end, he stood firm. However, his convalescence was a major ordeal—even though it was spent in luxury in Monaco. It's a time Donna would prefer to forget. 'At first Wayne was in a lot of pain, then he just became a pain,' she says. 'He was like a caged lion. He hated being handicapped, he hated being away from racing and he hated the thought that the other riders were getting on with the world championship without him. It really was a difficult period for him. And me . . . ,' she adds with a resigned smile.

Gardner's mood could hardly have been improved when he watched the Spanish GP on television—the first GP he'd missed since 1984. Lawson won—handed victory by Schwantz, who crashed when holding a big lead with just a few laps to go. Gardner had very mixed feelings as he sat watching a Rothmans Honda bike take victory while he sat at home with his leg in plaster from the knee down. However, there was little joy for Rothmans Honda in the succeeding races. In Italy, the leading riders boycotted the event because of the track conditions in the rain and Italian HB Honda rider Pirefrancesco Chili scored a hollow victory against a very depleted field. Rainey won the West German GP at Hockenheim with a clever last-lap passing move on Lawson, and Schwantz blitzed the field in Austria and Yugoslavia. At the halfway stage of the season, Rainey had a comfortable 13-point lead over Lawson in the championship chase, while the brilliant but erratic Schwantz had fallen by the wayside with his crashes in Australia and Spain costing him too many points. As things turned out, Rothmans Honda needn't have worried as Lawson used his considerable skill and experience to turn the screws on Rainey in the second half of the season. At the time, however, the situation didn't look so rosy. But if the Rothmans Honda camp was a little concerned, Marlboro Yamaha were desperate.

Lawson's surprise defection had left the team without a front-line rider, so team boss Giacomo Agostini had persuaded former Honda world champion Freddie Spencer to come out of retirement to fill the gap. The move was a dismal failure, with Spencer struggling to reproduce as much as a hint of his previous devastating form. Indeed, the team's only rostrum finish was a third place in Spain by the number two rider, Niall MacKenzie. Marlboro traditionally has been the biggest sponsor in GP motorcycle racing, and the team is used to success after three world championships with Lawson. Agostini needed to buy a rider for 1990 capable of bringing Marlboro the success it demanded, and one of the first doors he knocked on was Gardner's. Money wasn't a problem. Marlboro would be prepared to pay 'whatever it took' to get Gardner's signature. It would take at least $2 million, but Suzuki and the Italian Cagiva also entered the bidding.

'It was a funny situation to find myself in,' Gardner says. 'Here I was laid up with a broken leg and unable to ride, yet I had more teams chasing me than I had ever had before. It was weird. And there were some wild rumours flying around. I read in one magazine that Franco Uncini (the rider Gardner collided with in his first GP in 1983) was forming a new Suzuki team with Benetton as sponsor, and that I had signed as his rider. I immediately rang Harris (Barnett) and asked him if he knew somthing I didn't. I don't know where that rumour started, but I did get an approach from the Pepsi Suzuki team. However, I think they were only covering themselves in case Schwantz decided not to re-sign. The really serious offer came from Agostini.'

After staying away from the first few GPs while he had intensive theraphy on his injured leg, Gardner visited Hockenheim, Salzburg and Rijeka. It was at Rijeka for the Yugoslav GP that senior Honda officials, alarmed at the prospect he might defect to Yamaha, organised a meeting with Gardner. They brought in some big guns, including former Honda Racing Corporation director Yoichi Oguma. Gardner has enormous respect for Oguma-san, and had a close working relationship with him until he was moved to another department within Honda at the end of 1987. If anyone could convince Gardner to stay with Honda, it was his old friend Oguma-san. But there was considerable fence-mending to be done.

'It was quite a meeting,' Gardner recalls. 'I felt like an engine being tested on the dyno, with all the Japanese sitting around with notepads writing away in Japanese, like they were taking recordings from the engine. But it was good. I spilled my guts and told them exactly what I though of the whole situation— of Eddie joining Honda, the way it had happened, and what it had done to my riding. I told them they'd put me in a situation where my greatest competition was my own team-mate, and that it was one of the reasons I was sitting there with a broken leg— because I'd been riding over the top, feeling that I had to kick Eddie's arse every time we went out on the racetrack. I pointed out that having two champions in one team couldn't work. You just had to see how Alain Prost and Ayrton Senna were bitching at each other in the McLaren-Honda F1 car team. I laid all the cards on the table. Ago (Agostini) had been telling everyone he wanted to sign me for the next season, and the Honda bosses wanted to know if it was true. I told them it was, that Agostini was upset with his team's results this year, and that he was looking for a new rider and I'd received an offer which looked pretty good—a lot of money and the promise of good machinery. I told them another team was also interested and I'd be listening to all proposals and weighing them up. I also told them of a few of my other concerns, particularly over the development of the bike. I think it did some good. It certainly cleared the air.'

Gardner left the Honda bosses to ponder what he had said, and returned to Monaco to prepare for his comeback to racing at the Dutch Grand Prix. Claudio Costa had devised a stringent physiotherapy and exercise program, as well as a special electro-magnetic field treatment that hastened bone regeneration in his injured leg. The team had planned to allow Gardner to ease back into racing with a private test session at Snetterton in England a week before the Dutch GP, but Dr Costa vetoed it at the last minute. He wasn't completely happy with the leg and wanted Gardner to give it another week's rest. Gardner had the plaster cast removed at Dr Costa's mobile clinic at the track, and strapped on a lightweight, removable protective cast for the start of practice. 'I was pretty nervous before I went out for the first practice session. I knew Costa wouldn't let me ride if he had any doubts about the leg standing up to it, but it was still very painful and I was scared I would knock it or fall off and break it again. The cast was good protection, but it was also a constant reminder that I had a problem, and it was hard to concentrate on riding smoothly. It was pretty painful on the gearchanges, and I wasn't prepared to ride too hard. I kept getting stuck behind slower riders throughout qualifying because I wasn't prepared to dive under them on the corners.' Despite the problems, Gardner managed to qualify in ninth position, and said he was aiming for a top six position in the race. And that's how it turned out. Gardner rode a strong, steady race, dicing with Ron Haslam and MacKenzie for much of the time before upping the pace in the last few laps to almost catch Chili in fifth spot in a spirited, fairing-banging run to the chequered flag. His best lap, recorded near the finish, was 2:10.54 seconds—an improvement of 1.22 seconds over his qualifying time, and significantly, .7 seconds faster than the lap record he set when winning the Dutch GP the previous year.

The performance was quite remarkable considering that nine weeks earlier he had been laid up in hospital in America, with doctors saying it would be months before he walked again and at least six months before he raced a bike. 'Dr Costa did a fantastic job getting me fit for racing so quickly,' Gardner said after the race. 'It's great to be back racing again, and to do it so soon is a credit to the hard work Dr Costa put in. My leg stood up to the race really well, and I'm now confident that I can go on with the job in the Belgian GP next week. By the time we get to Le Mans for the French GP in three weeks I should be just about fully fit.' However, Gardner's optimism proved to be misplaced. The Belgian GP was a disaster, with the Spa-Francorchamps circuit a lot harder on his leg, with a lot more direction changes and hard braking points than Assen. He qualified in tenth spot, a disappointing three seconds off the pace, and admitted he was really struggling. But worse was to come early in the race, when one of his front discs exploded on one of the fastest sections of the track—a 280 kilometres per hour left-hand curve leading to the chicane. 'The front disc just exploded for no reason. I wasn't using the brakes, in fact I was flat out in sixth gear at the time. I can't help thinking I could have been killed if it had happened going into a corner where I had to brake hard. I'd never even heard of such a thing happening before, and there seemed to be no explanation. The disc just exploded, with fragments of steel going everywhere—even cutting through the mudguard and fairing. I panicked when it first happened because when I saw fragments explode from the front wheel I thought the front tyre must have burst. I looked down and saw what had happened and got the shock of my life. The carrier was just turning in the centre of the front wheel, with none of the disc left on it.' Gardner pulled out of the race immediately, and was badly shaken by the incident. He made his disgust quite obvious when he returned the bike to the Honda pit. A later investigation revealed that aluminium rivets the factory was experimenting with to hold the disc to the wheel hub had shifted loose and broken, allowing the disc to twist in the caliper and promptly shatter.

Lawson was eventually granted victory in the Belgian GP after farcical circumstances that saw the race halted twice because of rain, with the second re-start (won by Rainey) ruled invalid. Schwantz was awarded second place despite crashing after the second re-start, while Rainey was relegated top third.

Things went even worse for Gardner at Le Mans in the French GP. Once again, he struggled throughout qualifying then crashed after ten laps. His fierce pride was taking an awful battering, and after the race Gardner admitted it was one of the lowest points of his career. 'I just can't seem to get my mind into gear,' he lamented. 'There was no reason for me to crash, but everything I am trying to do at the moment seems to go wrong. I know I am not riding well, but the harder I try, the worse I seem to go. I wasn't coming out of the corner too fast, but the rear tyre slid then caught and high-sided me, I was worried I would damage my leg, but luckily I didn't, which was the only thing that went right for me all week.' While Gardner struggled, Lawson was superb, winning the race from Schwantz and Rainey in a consummate display that many saw as the turning point of the season. Although he had already won two GPs, the French race was the first time Lawson had really taken control and the victory set him up to attack Rainey's championship lead.

Gardner, meanwhile, headed for Japan and another tilt

at the Suzuka Eight-hour, hoping a return to his four-stroke racing boots on the RVF750 Honda he loves so much would help him to regain some confidence. It seemed to work, with Gardner and his team-mate Michael Doohan claiming pole position and leading for the first five hours as they shared riding duties on the machine. By then they had buit up a seemingly unbeatable one and a half lap lead. However, just before Doohan was to hand over the bike at the five-hour mark, he ran into the back of a slower rider and crashed the machine. Their race was over.

Honda used the opportunity of having Gardner in Japan to convince him to re-sign, and did a pretty good job. The HRC bosses convinced him of their continuing support and loyalty, and told him of planned changes to make the machines even more competitive in 1990. They also made some commitments towards Gardner's long-term future with Honda when his racing days were over, and threw in the carrot of the spectacular new Honda NSX sports car when it rolls of the assembly line. He didn't sign a contract, but the odds were shortening in Honda's favour.

Back in England the following weekend for the British Grand Prix, Gardner asked Phil Fearon to come to the track, hoping some input from the pyschologist would help him rebuild his shattered confidence. Once again, though, qualifying was disappointing and frustrating, with Gardner back in tenth spot on the grid as he tried to sort out a new chassis Honda had flown in from Japan for him. He did get a good start though, and was following Lawson through in fifth place when his engine went sour with an ignition failure. Gardner retired from the race, which was eventually won by Schwantz, with Lawson second and Rainey third. By this time the knockers had started to surface. Had Gardner 'lost his bottle?' they asked. Would he ever be able to get up there and race with the Americans again, or was he a has-been? Gardner was well aware of the doubts being expressed. However, it is not in his nature to quit. He asked his team to book Donington for the next day, and spent it working hard sorting out the new chassis, before heading off to Sweden for another GP there the next weekend.

Qualifying in Sweden started disastrously, with Gardner being brought down by a slow rider in the opening session.

Although he was unhurt, the crash wrecked the bike they had spent the previous Monday at Donington sorting out. His mechanics worked through the night to rebuild it, but the rest of the qualifying sessions were wet and Gardner was way back in twelfth spot on the grid, and highly embarrassed by his lowest-ever qualifying position. But the wheel of fortune finally turned Gardner's way in the race. He made a reasonable start and came through the field to fifth, where he settled down to strong and consistent lap times. The front-runners had bolted, and Gardner couldn't bridge the gap, but neither were they pulling away from him. For the first time since his comeback from injury, he was back on the pace. His reward came late in the race when Schwantz' Suzuki expired and Rainey crashed trying to challenge Lawson for the lead. Gardner took third behind Lawson and Christian Sarron and admitted it was a considerable relief to finally climb the rostrum again. 'It felt great. I had my share of luck with Wayne and Kevin dropping out, but it was about time some luck ran my way.' Rainey's crash virtually handed the world championship to Lawson. From being six and a half points clear, Rainey had dropped to thirteen and a half behind with just two races to go. The world title now looked beyond him.

Gardner also made one of the hardest decisions of his career at Sweden, although it wasn't made public until weeks after. After months wrestling with the problem, he decided his future lay with Honda and agreed to another two-year contract. The reasons were a complex mix, but the key elements included Gardner's belief that Honda, with its enormous resources, was more than capable of building the best bike for 1990; faith in the relationships he had with his technical staff—HRC engineer Tsunoda-san, team manager Stewart Shenton, Wilf Needham and the rest of his crew; Honda's commitment to his long-term future with the company; and a lucrative contract that was considerably more than he was getting in 1989, despite the disappointing year. He saw that, and the factory's decision to pay him his full retainer, as an act of good faith from Honda and was gratified by it and assurances about his status within HRC. There were two other elements too. One was a sense of unfinished business with Lawson. The American may have won round one of the battle to see who was the better rider, but the war wasn't over and it was important to Gardner that the duel be conducted on the same machines (although Honda had reacted to the sensitivity of the sitation by deciding to distance the two teams even more for 1990). And although Gardner would never admit to it, there was a fear about moving to a strange team with unfamiliar machinery and personnel, away from the comfortable associations he had built up over eight years with Honda and five years with Rothmans.

As if to celebrate the decision, Gardner and Lawson publicly buried the hatchet at a press conference at Anderstorp. Lawson said he had new respect for Gardner's talents after riding the Honda, and Gardner praised Lawson for the hard work he'd put in to overcome his initial problems adapting to the new bikes and to hit top form at such a crucial stage in the season. The pair then packed up and went to Czechoslovakia together for some private testing to prepare themselves for the GP there a fortnight later.

Gardner's misery continued in Czechoslovakia. Testing a new frame during qualifying, he was thrown off the bike and damaged his left leg again. In fact, he suffered a small fracture at one of the points where his leg had been broken so badly in April. Gardner didn't make known the extent of his new injury in case it sounded like an excuse to miss the race. Nevertheless, it was impossible to compete, and he reluctantly pulled out of the GP. He returned home to Monaco with his leg in a cast that had to stay on for another two weeks.

Few would have blamed him for missing the final GP in Brazil on 17 September, three weeks after Czechoslovakia, and it did cross his mind that it would be easier—and safer—to miss the last race. But Gardner has never taken the easy way. He knew he owed it to his team and his sponsors, but most of all to himself, to race in Brazil. 'I had to get back on the horse that bucked me,' he said. 'I had to race at Brazil to finish the season on a proper note—on the bike—not sitting at home watching the race on TV . . . so I could face the off-season testing program knowing I could get on with the job and get back up there again in 1990.

However, Gardner's commitment to racing didn't extend to taking any unnecessary risks in Brazil. He would not be able to improve on tenth position in the world championship, and considered it far more important to finish the race safely and without further damage to his leg. So while Eddie Lawson chalked up his fourth world title with second place behind Kevin Schwantz at Goiania, Gardner settled for seventh. Not that he enjoyed it. 'I hated riding around like that,' he said after the race. 'I got forced into the dirt at the end of the main straight by a rider I was trying to pass, and had a couple of moments with back-markers, and I just wasn't prepared to push any harder and risk a crash. I was relieved the season was finally over, to be honest. If someone had told me at the beginning that all those things would have happened to me, I wouldn't have believed it possible. It was a miserable year but I'm not through yet. I'll be back—you can count on that.'

And there is no doubt you can count on that. Gardner passionately believes he can win another world title and is determined to do it. When he sets his mind on achieving something, his determination is extraordinary.

There are still one or two dreams to come true before Wayne Gardner hangs up his helmet.